The

Ultimate Guide

to

SUCCESS

How to Achieve Your Goals in 10 Steps or Less

Dan McDaniel

Copyright © 2016 Dan McDaniel

All rights reserved.

ISBN-10: 1-533-68845-1

ISBN-13: 978-1-533-68845-3

Intellectual Property of Dan McDaniel Publishing

Cover design by Ida Fia Sveningsson; 3-D pyramid by Mykyta Zhdanov

Printed in the United States of America

This book is given to _____

from _____ because I care about
you and your greater success.

May this day, _____, _____, _____,
mark the beginning of your best year ever!

Download the audiobook for FREE!!

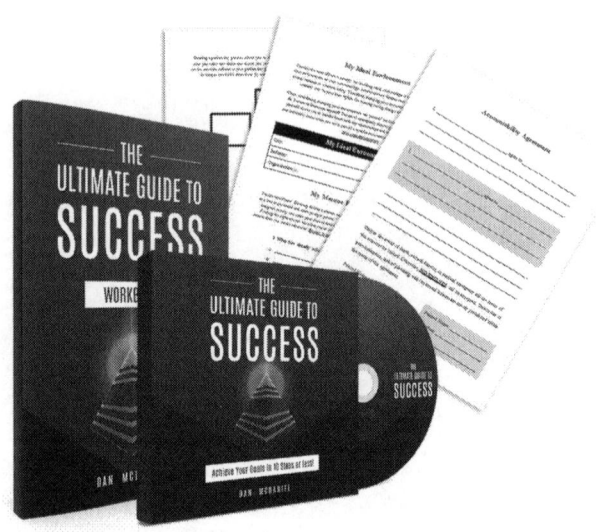

READ THIS FIRST

I have found that readers achieve their goals much faster when they use the companion workbook *as they read*. Gain access to *The Life You Want Workbook: A Companion to Dan McDaniel's The Ultimate Guide to Success* for a small fee and download the first 20 minutes of the audiobook 100% FREE by visiting the website below.

www.danmcdaniel.net/action

CONTENTS

Preface:

An Evening with Oprah

I met her exactly one year ago—on Saturday, October 18, 2014—in downtown Houston, Texas. Escorted by her appointed concierge, I was directed to a secure conference room. After enduring a very thorough "pat down" (and receiving a menacing glare from her security guard), we were finally in the same vicinity. I had locked eyes with Oprah Winfrey. Approaching with a shimmering smile and a greeting of glee, I received a humongous hug from the humble humanitarian. Casually dressed—avoiding the designer garments befitting of Hollywood royalty—she was wearing black denim jeans with coordinating boots, a gray top, and a beige leather jacket. Accessorizing with customized eyewear and O-shaped earrings, she sported her signature curls with extraordinary class and exceptional confidence. For she radiated with passion and gleamed with power. I could sense that sweet serenity was at the seat of her soul.

Fewer than 24 hours earlier, she had given the opening keynote of her fall 2014 U.S. speaking tour Oprah's The Life You Want Weekend. Designed to help attendees find their calling and fulfill their greatest potential, this two-day event inspired thousands of people from all across the world to blast past negativity and fearlessly step into the life that they were born to live. A magnetic speaker, Ms. Winfrey made all in attendance question their purpose.

An Evening with Oprah

"Why are you here?" asked Winfrey from the center stage of the jam-packed Toyota Center. She continued comically, "*I'm here* to help *you* figure out why you're here!" As I listened closely, lingering on her every word, I couldn't help but to be momentarily distracted by the A-list authors in attendance.

Just a few rows in front of me—also enjoying the luxury of VIP seating—were multiple *New York Times* bestselling authors and personal growth pioneers. Among these high-powered influencers were Houston native, research professor, and TEDx viral sensation **Brené Brown**; celebrated spiritual leader and host of the critically acclaimed Oprah Winfrey Network (OWN) series *Iyanla: Fix My Life*, **Iyanla Vanzant**; and the author of the self-reflective memoir-turned-global phenomenon *Eat, Pray, Love*, **Elizabeth Gilbert**.

While attending this glorious, potentially life-changing event, I was inspired to write my own book—not yet another memoir of self-discovery but, instead, a manual for living. *The Ultimate Guide to Success*—it would come to be called—would be my offering to the world, the expression of my purpose, and the manifestation of my soul. It is my hope that this book will do for you what Oprah's event did for me: **to see the possibilities of a new life** and, by applying the enclosed principles, to feel *empowered* to make your own vision a remarkable reality. It is my goal with *The Ultimate Guide to Success* to help you get closer to the life you want.

In her closing remarks, while explaining how quickly time passes, Oprah asked the audience a question that would—for the next 12 months—remain at the forefront of my psyche. Oprah asked us the following question as we frantically took notes in our newly-received yearly planners: "What will you have accomplished one year from now?" She continued, demonstrating with an on-screen time clock, how a year goes by "in a flash." Oprah wanted us to get clear about our vision. She wanted us to be able to articulate our proposed life changes within one year as a result of what we had learned at the conference.

Well, the year did, indeed, go by "in a flash." Six months into it, I was starting to feel like a complete failure. By the 12-month period, however, I had recovered. I had completed my book. The compilation of my life's learnings was now ready for distribution. To return the favor—and, hopefully, to get a similar result—I ask you the same question: **what will _you_ have accomplished one year from now?** In 365 days, will you be significantly closer to the life you want, or will you be hopelessly dreaming of a distant future where your life changes at its own accord? The choice is yours. Thankfully, though—by reading this book—I believe that you have made the right decision. Mark today's date on your calendar. For this just might be the first day of _**your best year ever!**_

Dan McDaniel
Sunday, October 18, 2015
12:36 A.M.

Introduction:

A Different Approach

"If there's a book that you want to read, but it hasn't been written yet, then you must write it."
—Toni Morrison

This assertion by novelist Toni Morrison perfectly explains why I decided to write this book. Before attending the Oprah event, I had grown frustrated with my own search for self-defined "success." I was a professional writer at age 19—writing books, editing manuscripts, and re-wording resumes—mostly for clients who would actually *pay me* for my services. It was the beginning of a dream—the seed of my ambition to become a world-renowned author. But I wasn't there yet. Young and ambitious, I began a nationwide search for the answer to the following question: **how can I go from where I am to where I want to be in the fastest, most effective way possible?**

In search for an answer to this question, I began reading books on the subject of success. I spent hours on Amazon.com and inside Barnes and Noble perusing the shelves for the manual to fulfillment, the new Bible of achievement, the ultimate guide to success—if you will—but to no avail. **Every book that I read failed to accurately describe the complete journey**

of achievement. One book would tell me to create a vision board but not tell me how to <u>execute</u> on that vision. Another book would tell me to "think big" but not explain to me that I was going to "fail big" along the way. An additional book would tell me a remarkable story about how the author had attained success but not how I, myself, could get the same results!

After years of navigating the maze of success, I have finally created my own roadmap. Within these pages are the principles that I have learned from years of research and experience. It is—proven by public opinion—**the most comprehensive book ever written on the subject of success**. It is *The Ultimate Guide to Success*—the book that I wish I had five years ago. To diminish your doubts, however, I have answered readers' top five most <u>frequently asked questions</u>.

1. What makes <u>you</u>, Dan McDaniel, qualified to write *The Ultimate Guide to Success*?

I believe that my role as the author of *The Ultimate Guide to Success* is to essentially be a journalist—to compile data from various sources into a completed work of nonfiction for the advancement of human achievement.

It is partly for this reason that, **over the past five years, I have spent nearly 5,000 hours studying the principles of success**. I have attended dozens of seminars, read hundreds of books, watched countless interviews, and spent hours of time speaking one-on-one with some of the world's most spiritually, physically, and financially successful people. Even the bibliography of this book—citing all of the magazine articles, newspaper clippings, biographies, documentaries, and academic studies reviewed—fails to accurately convey the amount of time and energy required to both peruse and produce such literature.

In addition to the aforementioned research, I have used the principles mentioned in *The Ultimate Guide to Success* to achieve goals in my own life. You may refer to my biography for specific accolades and achievements.

2. How is this book any <u>different</u> from every other book written about success?

The Ultimate Guide to Success is not just a book. It is **the most comprehensive book ever written on the subject of success**. Completing this book is the equivalent of receiving a Ph.D. from Success University! It thoroughly explains the science of success, the psychology of achievement, and the pain of personal transformation.

Unlike other popular books that simply tell you to "believe in yourself" or to "find your passion," this book actually shows you *how* to do those things. This way, you are not left wondering how to apply the proposed principles.

Another way that *The Ultimate Guide to Success* is different from other books within the marketplace is that it corresponds with an **interactive action guide**. This 20-page workbook contains a personalized perfect day planner (as explained in chapter one), a fill-in-the-blank daily habit tracker, a customizable immediate action agenda, and a state-of-the-art limiting beliefs eliminator. These tools—along with many others—can be instantly downloaded to your smartphone, your tablet, or your computer and printed out for immediate use by visiting **www.danmcdaniel.net/action**.

In addition to being both comprehensive and interactive, this book is also remarkably straightforward. It consists of brief chapters (averaging eight pages each) and easy-to-understand charts and graphs. Its total page count, in terms of core contents, is fewer than 100 pages. This means that you can avoid time-related stress by reading *The Ultimate Guide to Success* in six (6) hours or less!

3. From reading your book description, I understand that your book contains numerous <u>case studies</u>. Who are these selected individuals, and why did you decide to feature them in your book?

The Ultimate Guide to Success includes precisely 19 different case studies. I selected each individual based on *diversity*, *familiarity*, and *relevance* to the proposed success principle. You will, undoubtedly, recognize most of the names mentioned in this book; however, you will most likely have <u>not</u> heard their enclosed stories. The following is the complete list of individuals featured in this book (in order of appearance) and a brief description of how his or her story directly relates to achieving *your* specific goals:

1. **Criss Angel**, world-renowned magician and stuntman, achieved his childhood dream of becoming an internationally known illusionist after enduring over 20 years of self-discovery, failure, and rejection. His story demonstrates the importance of <u>having a clear vision</u> while experiencing multiple years of heart-wrenching hardship.

2. **Marie Forleo**, mega-rock star online entrepreneur, began building an eight-figure business while working multiple jobs. Her story illustrates how <u>being driven by necessity</u> allows you to transcend all barriers, all excuses, and all distractions while on the journey toward achieving your goals.

3. **Nicki Minaj**, multi-millionaire hip hop mogul, was driven to attain financial freedom as a result of her frustration with poverty. Her story illustrates how <u>having a strong purpose</u> consistently motivates you to achieve success.

4. **Taylor Swift**, award-winning recording artist, moved from Reading, Pennsylvania, to Nashville, Tennessee, in 2004 to pursue a career in music. Her story illustrates how <u>moving to a different location</u> can change the trajectory of your life.

5. **Tyra Banks**, fashion icon and television personality, moved to the fashion capital of the world, Paris, France, in 1991 to pursue a modeling career. Her story illustrates how <u>changing your environment</u> swiftly immerses you into the fountain of your dreams.

6. **Arnold Schwarzenegger**, bodybuilder and actor, moved from Austria to America in 1968 to escape his impoverished home country and become a star. His story illustrates how <u>relocating to a different country</u> can propel you toward the life you want.

7. **Tim Ferriss**, rock star bestselling author and investor, began building a world-class network of mentors by volunteering for a non-profit startup. His story illustrates how you can go from no connections and very little money to establishing personal relationships with influencers by <u>offering free help</u>.

8. **Charlie Hoehn**, author and entrepreneur, used a very persuasive email to gain the friendship and the mentorship of one of his biggest role models. His story illustrates how <u>helping people achieve *their* goals</u> can actually help you achieve your own.

9. **Ryan Holiday**, author and media strategist, leveraged his college job as a journalist to land an internship with a book publishing powerhouse. His story illustrates how <u>pursuing an apprenticeship</u> can lead to career-defining opportunities.

10. **John Lee Dumas**, entrepreneur and Internet radio show host, took his company from zero profit to over $200,000 per month in revenue after just slightly more than 18 months in business. His story demonstrates the importance of <u>getting a mentor</u> so that you can experience meteoric growth.

A Different Approach

11. **Vishen Lakhiani**, socially-conscious entrepreneur and personal growth pioneer, quadrupled his company's revenue in just four years. His story demonstrates the importance of <u>joining mastermind groups</u> and <u>connecting with smart people</u> to rapidly grow your business and/or yourself.

12. **Suze Orman**, rock star financial advisor and bestselling author, went from making $400 per month as a waitress at age 29 to producing more than $10,000 per month as a financial advisor at age 30. Her story illustrates how <u>establishing empowering beliefs</u> can take you from a history of scarcity to a future of abundance.

13. **Big Sean**, hip hop recording artist, landed a record deal after ignoring all previous obligations to frantically drive to a radio station and rap for hip hop royalty. His story demonstrates the importance of <u>taking *immediate* action</u> during moments of rare opportunity.

14. **Colin Wright**, entrepreneur and full time traveler, utilized strategic thinking to go from 12-hour workdays at an office to full time travel in multiple countries around the world. His story illustrates how <u>creating an action plan</u> can rapidly move you in the direction of your goals.

15. **Chris Guillebeau**, full time traveler and bestselling author, developed a system to write 300,000 words per year by simply writing 1,000 words per day. His story illustrates how <u>developing positive habits</u> can create long-lasting success.

16. **Jennifer Lopez**, multi-faceted entertainment icon, went from sleeping on a bench in a dance studio to landing career-defining movie roles to breaking records as a recording artist in just over a decade. Her story illustrates the importance of <u>gaining momentum</u> so that you can enjoy the so-called "lucky" breaks and life-changing opportunities that result from relentlessly pursuing your goals.

17. **Oprah Winfrey**, media proprietor, spent precisely 16 years—literally half her life, at that time—in the broadcasting industry before her television show became a national phenomenon. Her story illustrates how <u>practicing patience</u> allows you to master your craft and manifest your destiny.

18. **Kanye West**, music icon and connoisseur of controversy, persevered through a life-threatening medical emergency to gain elite status in the recording industry. His story illustrates how <u>practicing persistence</u> ultimately leads to a well-deserved victory.

19. **Tyler Perry**, media mogul and world-renowned playwright, endured bouts of homelessness and six years of failure before producing a successful play. His story illustrates how <u>changing your approach</u> and <u>enduring heart-wrenching failure</u> propel you forward while creating the life you truly want.

4. Will reading this book guarantee that I get <u>the life I want</u>?

No, the act of solely reading this book will not get you the results that you want; however, <u>applying the principles</u> written within this book, i.e., actually *doing something* with this information, can greatly increase your odds of living the life of your dreams.

Furthermore (to be completely honest), you could put everything you have into achieving a goal—every bit of strength in your body and every ounce of passion in your soul—and *still* not achieve it. It happens all the time. Thousands of unfamiliar stories of relatively unknown people exist as the result of single-minded ambition and laser-focused desire. For the truth is: **you *could* possibly achieve your dreams, and you *could* possibly crash and burn and never fully recover.** It is up to you, however, to determine if the proposed risk is worth it.

My intention in writing this book is to instill a sense of hope and possibility within you while simultaneously maintaining a perspective of harsh reality. My ultimate goal is that these ten (10) steps get you the results that you want.

5. Dan, stop it with the B.S. Just tell me the 10 steps already!

Well, that's not exactly a question, but okay… First of all, you need to be patient (step 8). Secondly, telling you the ten (10) steps in advance won't help you very much. It is really <u>the steps *within* the steps</u> that lead to personal transformation. The overall process of goal achievement is what creates the results. For a brief summary of what you will learn in each chapter, however, refer to the following overview:

<u>Chapter 1: Vision</u>

In chapter one, you will discover how to create a clear vision for your future. You will learn the difference between why you may *think* you want to become a millionaire and why you may *really* want to become a millionaire. In this chapter, I will explain how to recognize the <u>true motive</u> of your ambitions and how to define a life of fulfillment on your own terms. In addition to learning how to define (or, perhaps, *refine*) your goals, you will also discover:

- The true definition of success (hint: it's not what you think).

- **The five (5) questions to discover your life's purpose.**

- The secret to experiencing the life you want (even before you actually have it).

<u>Chapter 2: Purpose</u>

In chapter two, you will discover the importance of having a strong purpose. You will also learn how to distinguish between a strong purpose and a weak purpose. In this chapter, I will explain how to attain <u>the ultimate trifecta of motivation</u>. In addition to learning how to both manufacture and maintain the essential drives of human nature, you will also discover:

- The three (3) layers of purpose (and how to use them to your advantage).

- The three (3) enemies of achievement (and how to overcome them).

- **The #1 secret to eliminating procrastination, excuses, and overall laziness for the rest of your life!**

Chapter 3: Relationships

In chapter three, you will discover the importance of building solid relationships. You will also learn how changing your environment can directly change your life. In this chapter, I will reveal some of the world's most powerful techniques for penetrating seemingly "untouchable" social networks and getting into the hearts and minds of high achievers. In addition to learning how to build solid relationships, you will also discover:

- **The #1 factor that determines your income, your health, and your overall level of happiness.**

- How to get a mentor (even when you feel like you have nothing to offer).

- The top secret strategy for networking with "untouchable" celebrities like Oprah Winfrey.

Chapter 4: Beliefs

In chapter four, you will discover how to establish empowering beliefs. This means that you will learn how to transform pain from your past into fuel for your future. In this chapter, I will help you identify the thoughts and the stories that are holding you back from achieving your goals. In addition to learning how to establish empowering beliefs, you will also discover:

- The three (3) key factors that determine your <u>subconscious</u> beliefs.

- **The <u>one question</u> that reveals all of your <u>hidden</u> beliefs.**

- The five-step process for overcoming your <u>limiting</u> beliefs and re-programming your mind for success.

<u>Chapter 5: Action</u>

In chapter five, you will discover the importance of taking *immediate* action. You will also learn how to create an action plan that helps you achieve your goals much faster than you would otherwise. In this chapter, I will unveil what is possibly the fastest way to get from where you are to where you want to be. In addition to exploring the benefits of immediate action, you will discover:

- **The #1 cause of fear (and how to overcome it).**

- The one question that always leads to immediate action.

- The simple, 3-step framework that allows you to challenge conventional thinking and accelerate your success.

<u>Chapter 6: Habits</u>

In chapter six, you will discover how to develop positive habits. You will learn how to form unconscious patterns of behavior that help you achieve your goals. Throughout this chapter, I will explain how small, seemingly insignificant choices add up over time. In addition to learning how to develop positive habits, you will also discover:

- How to make achieving your goals practically inevitable.

- How to break down your yearly goals into daily milestones.

– The <u>one habit</u> highly regarded as "the common denominator of success."

Chapter 7: Momentum

In chapter seven, you will discover how to gain momentum. You will learn how to move toward your goals at a rapid pace. In this chapter, I will describe the experience of being overwhelmed with opportunity. In addition to learning how to gain momentum, you will also discover:

– How to experience the elusive phenomenon known as "overnight success."

– **The truth about so-called "lucky" breaks and life-changing opportunities.**

– The secret to achieving your wildest dreams in record time.

Chapter 8: Patience

In chapter eight, you will discover how to properly prepare for success before momentum takes effect. You will learn how to arrive at achievement with a humble heart and a wise spirit. In this chapter, I will explain how to acquire the essential characteristic of patience. In addition to learning how to be patient while on the journey toward achieving your goals, you will also discover:

– Why multiple years of apprenticeship are the keys to lifelong achievement.

– **How the slow process of mastering your craft prepares you for the fast process of immediate opportunity.**

– How a lifetime of work can lead to one moment of supreme destiny.

Chapter 9: Failure

In chapter nine, you will learn how to cope with failure. You will discover how the lessons of failure actually prepare you for success. In this chapter, I will explain how **falling flat on your face** can actually work in your favor. In addition to learning how to cope with failure, you will also discover:

- Why failure should be expected rather than avoided.

- **How to turn your <u>adversity</u> into your <u>advantage</u>.**

- How to navigate devastating disappointments and soul-crushing setbacks.

Chapter 10: Persistence

In chapter ten, you will learn how to practice persistence. You will discover how to continue on your journey of achievement even during moments of extreme difficulty. In this chapter, I will explain how to harness your internal tenacity and continuously move forward even in the face of tremendous opposition. In addition to learning how to practice persistence, you will also discover:

- **The <u>real</u> purpose of hardship (and how to benefit from its experience).**

- How to remain focused on your goals (even during moments of temporary defeat).

- The secret to navigating medical emergency and financial crisis when all you want to do is give up.

These ten (10) elements—vision, purpose, relationships, beliefs, action, habits, momentum, patience, failure, and persistence—are all vital components of the <u>ultimate success formula</u>. It is the strategic alignment of these components, however, that ultimately creates the results that you want. **Continue on to <u>Step 1</u> to begin your journey toward massive achievement.**

Step 1:

Decide what you want.

      The first step in the process of achieving your goals is deciding what you want. When you have a clear vision of the life you desire, you are then equipped to create a plan of action that gets you closer to your proposed destination. Imagine boarding a plane with a pilot who has no idea where he is going. You wake up before dawn, pack your bags, put on your best suit, and drive down to the airport. After going through the security clearance and boarding the plane, you realize that the pilot has no recollection of the plane's destination. "So... where are we headed?" says the pilot over the intercom. You begin to shrivel with fear as your fellow passengers riot in frenzy.

      "You don't know where we're going? But you're the pilot!" yells a worried passenger. "Oh, yes. I'm sorry..." replies the pilot. "Destination: Mediocre Ville, Utah – Home of The Average and The Ordinary. It's the most popular destination for tourists. Its main attractions include Conformity Palace and Comfort Plaza. How could I have forgotten?" says the pilot. "We are scheduled to arrive in three hours."

      For this is life without a clear vision. Chaotic, capricious, and caressed by confusion. The only way to avoid the flight to Mediocre Ville is to know exactly what you want. The road to success begins with a decision to create the life you truly desire.

What is success, anyway?

Here's the truth: <u>Success is living life in alignment with your values</u>. It is about discovering who you are and defining what really matters to *you*. Once you truly understand yourself, your vision will become clear and your values will reflect your true heart's desire. According to British self-improvement sensation Paul McKenna, we define our values based on what our goals will *give* us.

For example, **you may think you want to become a millionaire** so that you can quit your job and travel the world. But what you might *really* want is a deeper sense of freedom, adventure, and meaning. In your mind, becoming a millionaire may seem like the only path toward creating the freedom you so desire. In reality, however, there are numerous ways to experience frequent adventure and perpetual meaning in your life without having a million dollars in the bank. The money is simply a means of receiving your end goal of complete freedom.

> *"Success is not the result of making money. Making money is the result of success."*
>
> —Earl Nightingale, *The Strangest Secret*

In the end, your desire for success is fueled by the psychological need to feel good. You want to become a millionaire so that you can *feel* free. You want to write a book so that you can *feel* significant. You want to be in a relationship so that you can *feel* like you're not alone. You want to lose weight so that you can *feel* desirable, confident, and sexy!

Your goal is solely determined by which *feeling* it will give you at the time of its achievement. In order to understand which feelings you want to experience, you must first understand your values.

Understand Your Values

Your core values determine what *really* matters to you. They identify the truth of your often-unknown desires—your hopes, your dreams, and your internal ambitions. Essentially, your values are the core essence of your soul's desire. They are the driving force of your behavior and the master architect of your aspirations. Understanding your values is the foundation of success. It allows you to ignite your passion and unleash your potential. Creating the life you want begins with your answering the following five questions:

1. **What would you do if you had no limitations?** If you had no chance of failing and unlimited resources—an abundance of time, money, energy, and relationships—what would you do with your life? What would you experience? How would you grow? How would you contribute? Envision your ideal life five years into the future, independent of other people's expectations, judgments, and/or imposed beliefs about who you are and what you do. For this is the life you truly want. The experiences and the emotions that you envision are what truly matter to you. The _feelings_ that you are currently envisioning are what you truly desire.

2. **When are you most happy?** Identifying the times when you are most happy will help you understand at which moments you experience the greatest joy and fulfillment. Peak experiences such as spending time with your family, speaking on stage, and/or winning a state championship identify your most fond memories and expose your ulterior desires for common psychological needs such as connection, significance, and achievement. Identifying when you are most happy is one of the best ways to identify your values.

3. **What would you do for free?** Identifying the activities that you would do for free is the key to unlocking your passion and understanding your values. In fact, discovering what you would _pay_ to do is an even better indicator of your subconscious desires. Reflect on the activities that you would do for free and discover the path that is meant for you.

4. **What comes easily to you but hard to others?** Taking the time to explore what comes easily to you but hard to others is a great way to discover your natural talents. Reflect on the topics on which people ask for your advice.

Think about all of the times in which people have asked for your help. On which subject(s) did you provide expertise? What skill(s) do you possess that make your peers look to you as an authority? Discover what comes easily to you and begin on your journey toward the life you were born to live.

     5. _For what are you willing to suffer?_ Here's the truth: the road to success is very long and difficult, full of chastising challenges, heart-wrenching hardships, and devastating disappointments. Therefore, you must ensure that the life you want is worth the inevitable pain and suffering. When you live life in alignment with your values, you ultimately realize that it is all worth it. Continue reading to discover how to endure the painstaking journey toward the life you so desperately want.

Have a Clear Vision

"In my deepest, darkest moments, what saved me was a vision."
—Iyanla Vanzant

     The way to endure the inevitable pain and suffering that comes with creating the life you want is to have a clear vision. When failure and disappointment are the *temporary* results of your labor, your vision will pull you forward. Allow your answers to the aforementioned questions to help you craft a mental picture of your ideal life. You must be able to see, hear, and feel the life you want long before you ever create it. For your vision will allow you to see beyond your present-day circumstances and step into a new world of infinite possibilities.

     But how do you create a vision? How do you form a mental picture of the life you want *before* you actually have what you want? Well, this is how: Close your eyes and imagine that your life is perfect within the next 2-3 years. Imagine your perfect day and the events that take place hour-by-hour. In which city do you live? At what time do you wake up? With whom do you meet throughout the day? What do you spend most of your time doing? This is a portrait of your ideal day, which will allow you to create a vision for your ideal life.

The Ultimate Guide to Success by Dan McDaniel

"The only thing worse than being blind is having sight but no vision."
—Helen Keller

With the intention of providing a clear outline (and to satisfy your curiosity), here is a portrait of my ideal day:

05:00 A.M. – Wake up in high-rise apartment located in downtown Portland, Oregon, United States
05:30 A.M. – Visualize the achievement of long-term goals
05:45 A.M. – Review schedule for the day
06:00 A.M. – Run two (2) miles at the local park
06:30 A.M. – Practice yoga with spouse
07:00 A.M. – Eat healthy breakfast with spouse
07:30 A.M. – Write 500-1,000 words of upcoming book
12:00 P.M. – Have lunch with group of friends
01:00 P.M. – Check personal email; discover that I passively made $500 USD via automated marketing campaigns
01:15 P.M. – Meet with executive assistant
01:30 P.M. – Schedule interview with Oprah
01:45 P.M. – Approve tour dates for 8-city speaking tour
02:00 P.M. – Plan out product launch sequence
04:00 P.M. – Interview entrepreneur for *The Dan McDaniel Show*
05:00 P.M. – Have weekly Skype call with high-end client
06:00 P.M. – Read 10 pages of *The Autobiography of Benjamin Franklin*
07:00 P.M. – Have dinner/date with spouse
10:00 P.M. – Go to bed

As you can see from my perfect day portrait, a few of my top priorities are fitness, connection, and creation. As long as I fulfill those three basic needs, happiness and fulfillment take care of themselves. Creating a portrait of your ideal day allows you to affirm your top priorities. It shows you what you really care about and allows you to synthetically experience the life of your dreams. **You may refer to the personalized perfect day planner found at www.danmcdaniel.net/action to create your own perfect day portrait.**

After you have created your perfect day portrait, answered the five questions to discover your purpose, and formed your own definition of success based on your top values, you should now have a clear vision of the life you want. It is this vision that will pull you forward in the midst of the chaos and the confinement known as your current reality. Let's take a look at how Criss Angel successfully attained his vision despite many years of pain-staking self-discovery and heart-wrenching hardship.

Case Study: Criss Angel

Born Christopher Sarantakos, Criss Angel is a world-famous magician who has always dreamed of becoming a superstar. At age seven, Criss was fascinated by a card trick, and his life changed forever. The card trick had been shown to him by his aunt, and it left a lasting impression. "It mesmerized me... It had this profound effect on me, and I wanted to know how she did it," Criss reflected.

"I drove everybody nuts showing them this card effect that I had learned." A few years later, Criss received a magic set for Christmas. This only further prompted him to learn more about the science of illusion. For magic fueled his curiosity. Reflecting on his love for illusion, Criss said, "I was enchanted by it... It just took me to a whole different place—a place of endless possibilities."

Fascinated by the allure of illusion, Criss would reportedly turn his parents' living room into a magic show. In fact, childhood friends recall him accidentally lighting his mother's rug on fire while performing a magic trick! For he was obsessed to the brink of destruction. Formal education couldn't even penetrate Criss' eagerness to learn magic. Criss recalls, "Even in school, I wanted to leave early so that I could go home and work on magic."

Eager to share his passion, Criss began performing on stage at age 14. He would perform at local restaurants in front of families for free. "I just wanted to perform," said Criss. "I didn't care if I performed for free. Small groups. Large groups. It didn't matter." Criss would reportedly spend all of his tips at a local magic shop, purchasing the latest magic kits as an investment in his career. Exhibiting a rather unique blend of courage, stupidity, and foresight, Criss once jumped from the rooftop to the hedges of his childhood home envisioning that he was a "world-famous stuntman." For even young, idealistic Criss had no idea just how real his vision would become.

At age 17, Criss had graduated high school and was now free to follow his dreams. He decided to forego college and, instead, pursue magic. When asked about this decision, Criss replied, "My college was going out there and doing it in the real world... making mistakes and figuring things out." For Criss couldn't imagine life without magic. This is what he had to say when reflecting on this major life decision to pursue a career in magic:

"What I could visualize for myself was the only thing that I was obsessed with and spent my time doing literally seven days per week, fifteen to eighteen hours per day. Magic was all I ever thought about. It's all I ever did."

In pursuit of his dreams, Criss formed his own local television show on a cable access station. Reflecting on this experience, Criss said, "I produced it, created it, wrote it, and starred in it. It was really my first endeavor in having a television series—even though it was at the local level." Totally convinced that he would become a superstar, Criss would practice writing his signature on the walls of his parents' basement. For he had an inner knowing—years before he had been discovered—that he would be a star.

The next two decades of Criss' career consisted of many years of self-discovery, epic failure, and sheer rejection. During this time, Criss experienced everything from leading musical groups to losing his father to cancer. From 1998 to 2001, he performed on the streets of New York City experiencing constant rejection by studio executives while trying to finance a big budget magic show. Criss was in such dire need for cash that he convinced his mother to refinance her home in order for him to produce the magic show. Thankfully, the show was a massive success!

Criss' 65-minute stage show *Mindfreak* debuted on October 31, 2007. The success of that Halloween show brought him new-found fame and much-needed publicity. The true tipping point in his career, however, came in August 2002 when he survived 24 hours inside a sealed water chamber, astounding television audiences worldwide. Although he reportedly suffered from dehydration and exhaustion, his childhood dream was finally coming true. At this point, Criss was 34 years old and had been performing live for over 20 years! The world had finally taken notice.

On July 20, 2005, the television series *Criss Angel: Mindfreak* debuted with immense public acclaim. By the third season of the show, Criss had become a bonafide superstar. Fulfilling his vision of becoming a "world-famous stuntman" with his own television show, Criss floated above the luxurious hotel Luxor Las Vegas atop the brightest beam of light in the world. For he shined like a star while fans from around the globe watched live 350 feet below. Through consistent action and unbridled persistence, Criss had achieved his childhood dreams. For this is the result of having a clear vision.

Select Your Most Important Goal

Now that you have created a clear vision for your life, you are in the position to select your most important goal. Selecting your most important goal allows you to avoid scattering your resources, i.e., your time, your money, and your energy, by focusing on the one goal that will get you closer to your vision. You may begin this process by writing down five (5) goals that you would like to accomplish over your lifetime. From this list, choose the one goal that, if achieved, would have the greatest positive impact on your life. For this is the goal that will ignite your enthusiasm and empower your ambition. With the intention of providing a practical example of this concept, here is a list of five common goals:

1. Lose weight
2. Travel the world
3. Write a book
4. Make more money
5. Start a business

In this example, I have circled "make more money" because achieving this one goal will make the other goals more attainable. The act of making more money will give you the financial reserves that allow you to buy healthier foods (in order to lose weight), hire an editor (for your book), book more flights (so that you can travel), and purchase accounting software (for your business). Achieving the singular goal of making more money would give you the resources to achieve all of the other goals. This does not mean that money will solve all of your problems (in fact, it may cause even more problems). It simply means that making more money is the one most important goal in this particular example.

Be Specific

Now that you have selected your most important goal, you must ensure that your goal is specific. Your goal must be measurable and time-sensitive. Having a deadline on a specific goal allows you to track your progress and measure your growth. Take a look at the graph below to understand the difference between goals that are specific and goals that are not specific.

Not Specific		Specific
Lose weight	→	Lose 30 pounds in six (6) months
Travel the world	→	Visit 25 different countries within the next two (2) years
Write a book	→	Write a nonfiction self-improvement book that helps 10,000 people
Make more money	→	Make an extra $1,000 per month within the next three (3) months
Start a business	→	Get my first customer within the next four (4) weeks

Ensuring that your one most important goal is specific makes you one step closer to achieving your dreams. Understanding your values and outlining your perfect day ensures that you are on track toward getting what you *really* want. Continue on to the next chapter to discover the three (3) biggest obstacles to achieving your goals (and how to overcome them).

Step 2:

Have a strong purpose.

"He who has a why to live can endure almost any how."
—Friedrich Nietzsche

In his *New York Times* bestselling book *Drive: The Surprising Truth About What Motivates Us*, Daniel Pink explains that purpose is one of the top three drives of human nature. Drawing on nearly four decades of scientific research, Pink discovered that purpose and meaning are the cornerstones of the human experience. This research proves that having a strong purpose will give you the physiological strength and the psychological fortitude to endure even the harshest of conditions. Having a deep sense of purpose and meaning will allow you to navigate the mental and emotional warfare known as the journey toward creating the life you want.

In his memoir *Man's Search for Meaning*, Viktor Frankl illustrated how purpose and meaning directly impact the direction of our lives. He described from first-hand experience how survivors of the Holocaust endured such harsh conditions. Despite constant suffering in concentration camps, the prisoners who survived all had a really strong *reason* to live. Whether it was to simply re-connect with their loved ones or to ultimately live to tell the story, prisoners

11

who survived found *meaning* in their suffering. That strong sense of purpose and meaning was the only thing that got them through.

On the journey toward creating the life of your dreams, you must have a strong purpose. For it is this purpose that will help you avoid procrastination, burn-out, and feelings of despair. For it is this purpose that will help you break through barriers and live the life you truly want.

How do I know when I have a strong purpose?

You know that you have a strong purpose when you decide that **nothing is going to stop you**. When you consciously decide that only the inevitability of death can inhibit your progress, then you have a strong enough purpose. In other words, you will either achieve your goals or die trying. When you allow only the events of natural disaster or medical emergency to *temporarily* inhibit the progression of your destiny, then you know that you are living life on purpose. A desire this deep will ignite your passion and reveal superhuman capabilities that are shocking to both you and everyone in your circle of influence. The following are a few examples of a strong purpose:

Weak purpose: "I want to lose weight."

Strong purpose: "I *must* lose 30 pounds of fat within the next six (6) months or else I will die from a heart attack and leave my wife and infant children in financial ruin and emotional distress."

Weak purpose: "I should quit my job."

Strong purpose: "I *must* quit my soul-sucking job within the next 12 months or else I will end up miserable, depressed, and full of regret because I never followed my heart."

Weak purpose: "I need to make more money."

Strong purpose: "I *must* make an extra $1,000 per month within the next six (6) months or else I will not be able to eat or pay rent, which will result in my starvation and homelessness for an indefinite amount of time."

As you can see from the examples above, a strong purpose has special criteria. While a weak purpose is somewhat vague and uninspiring, a strong purpose is a) specific b) time-sensitive, and c) consequential. Your purpose must consist of a specific result attained by a certain deadline with clear consequences for lack of achievement. For this will be the fuel for your passion and your armor against the three enemies of achievement.

The 3 Enemies of Achievement

The three enemies of achievement are comfort, conformity, and cowardice. As stated in my first book *Extreme Honesty*, "It is the pursuit of comfort, the custom of conformity, and the coercion of cowardice that write the story of your enslavement." For it is only through consistent courage supported by the foundation of purpose that will set you on the path toward living the life of your dreams. But, in order for you to successfully defend yourself against these three enemies, you must first seek to understand them. For this is why the following paragraphs will explain to you each enemy, in order of its influence over human psychology.

The number one enemy of achievement is comfort. Comfort is defined as, "a state of physical ease and freedom from pain or constraint." Well, the journey toward the life you want is the exact opposite of that! The odyssey of self-actualization is the antithesis of pain-free! In fact, it is one of the most painful experiences that you will ever endure. The good news is that **your short-term pain is in direct proportion to your long-term pleasure**. The more you risk comfort in the present, the more you guarantee fulfillment in the future.

The second enemy of achievement is conformity. Conformity is defined as, "behavior in accordance with socially accepted conventions or standards." It is the act of complying with the pre-established "rules" of society. Conformity is often described as "herd mentality," the act of doing what everyone else is doing. When you conform, you get lost in the crowd. You lose your identity and get recruited into a life of mediocrity. For true success and fulfillment stem from authentic self-expression and the innate desire for mastery. In the words of Earl Nightingale, "To be great at anything is to be a nonconformist."

The third enemy of achievement is cowardice, or lack of courage. Cowardice is a form of fear. It is the inability to demonstrate strength of character during a challenge. Cowardice may reveal itself when you are struggling with a moderate (or an extreme) level of adversity. Cowardice shows up during the climb to the mountaintop. It appears during your walk through the valley. When cowardice shows up during your journey toward the life you want, you must consciously choose courage. For this is the only way to reach the next peak. You must continue to move forward even in the face of tremendous fear and uncertainty. But how do you move forward? How do you choose courage over cowardice when things get difficult? Well, that all begins with being driven by at least one of the three layers of purpose: passion, frustration, or necessity.

The 3 Layers of Purpose

The three layers of purpose are a group of fundamental drives that inspire change in an individual. Igniting one of these three drives, or "layers," will inspire even the most lethargic individual. The conscious manipulation of these drives will result in decreased procrastination while increasing your capacity for world domination. Igniting at least one of these three layers of purpose is the secret to eliminating your BS excuses and perpetuating your vision out into the world. The ultimate trifecta of motivation occurs when you are driven by all three layers of purpose. **When you are simultaneously _passionate_ about what you do, _frustrated_ with your current reality, and motivated by the trigger of _necessity_, then you are in the perfect position to succeed.** Let's take a look at how these three human drives manifest through the lives of real people.

"Turn your 'shoulds' into your 'musts.' Change occurs due to necessity."
—Tony Robbins

The first layer of purpose is necessity, the act of being absolutely necessary. When something is absolutely necessary—like food, water, or shelter—our survival instincts are triggered. We, as animals, leverage all of our resources (i.e., time, money, relationships, etc.) to ensure that the essential needs of life are provided. It is this drive of necessity that pushes us past our perceived limits and catapults us into massive action.

When mega-rock star online entrepreneur Marie Forleo was asked how she got her business off the ground while working multiple jobs, she replied, "What really helped me in the beginning was that, **by necessity**, I was super busy. I bartended every night, and I worked as a personal assistant." Marie continued, "**I had to feed myself.** I had to pay rent, so I couldn't take my foot off the gas." The power of necessity transcends all barriers, excuses, and distractions. When used correctly, it can be **the single most powerful tool for achieving your goals**.

The second layer of purpose is frustration. When you are sick and tired of being a victim of your circumstances, *then* you will be compelled to take action. Before you can alter your behavior, however, the pain of staying the same must be greater than the pain of change. For it is only when your current circumstances become unbearable that you are motivated to act. Let's take a look at how international rap sensation Nicki Minaj was driven by her frustration with poverty.

Case Study: Nicki Minaj

"When I was a little girl, I would pray to God, 'Please make me rich so that I can take care of my mom.'"
—Nicki Minaj

Born Onika Maraj (pronounced ō-nē'-kŭ → mŭ-rŏg), Nicki Minaj grew up in the poverty-stricken neighborhoods of Jamaica, Queens, New York. After leaving her birth island of Trinidad when she was a little girl, Nicki Minaj and her family moved to the northeastern region of the United States with the intention of creating a better life for themselves. Unfortunately, however, their plans backfired. Instead of creating a better life for his family, Nicki's father fell victim to the 1980s crack epidemic and drug culture of New York. Years later, Nicki recalled seeing vials of crack on the sidewalk as she walked home from school.

Her father's addiction eventually escalated into violent outbursts and destructive bouts of rage. According to her 2011 interview on _The Ellen DeGeneres Show_, her father's behavior had once become so destructive that he attempted to kill Nicki's mother by setting their house on fire. Although her mother made it out of the house safely, this event engrained a deep sense of helplessness within the heart of young Nicki. It was in that moment when her sole purpose in life became to help her mother by becoming rich.

In an exclusive interview with Ray Daniels of A-105 Radio, Nicki said, "When I was a little girl, I would pray to God, 'Please make me rich so that I can take care of my mom.'" Nicki continued as she reflected on her drug-infested upbringing, "I never want my children or my children's children to grow up in that type of environment."

This frustration with poverty drove Nicki to create a grand vision for herself and for her family's future. It was Nicki's desire to end her family's financial struggle that fueled her ambition and drove her to attain financial freedom. Coupled with a passion for music and the insatiable desire to succeed, Nicki's deep sense of purpose resulted in undeniable certainty concerning her future. The following is possibly one of the greatest predictions of success in recorded human history. It occurred in a 2008 interview with _MEE Magazine_. When asked about her vision of the future, Nicki replied with the following:

> _"Five years from now, I see myself being a multi-millionaire/mogul with an all-girl empire. You can listen to all of my music to understand why I am about to become the new and improved queen of rap."_

Less than five years later, her prediction had come true! By 2013, Nicki Minaj had become one of the most influential entertainers of all time. Sitting atop her multi-million-dollar empire, she had been crowned by the masses as the queen of rap, establishing herself as a business mogul with a legacy that will last a lifetime. Even more important than her professional pursuits is the realization that Nicki achieved her _real_ goal—to become financially independent so that she can take care of her family.

During a trip back home to Trinidad, the childhood story of Nicki Minaj came full circle in 2010. Shortly before the debut of her first album *Pink Friday*, Nicki Minaj bought her mother a new home. While forever remembering that her childhood home was burned down during her father's drug-induced rage, this new home symbolized a new beginning. A new chapter in the lives of Nicki and her family. This new home symbolized the ending of struggle and the beginning of freedom.

While reflecting on this experience in her MTV documentary *Nicki Minaj: My Time Now*, Nicki said, "My happiness doesn't come from money or fame. My happiness comes from seeing life without struggle." Well, the struggle is over. Because of her drive to succeed, Nicki's family will never have to worry about money again. Nicki Minaj's vision came true, and she is now the provider that she has always dreamed of becoming. For this is the result of being driven by frustration.

The third layer of purpose is passion. Passion is the heart, the soul, and the core essence of a strong purpose. When you are passionate about a career, a cause, or a calling, you are driven to move mountains and break barriers in the pursuit of your goal. You are willing to do whatever it takes to get where you want to be because your drive comes from within. When you are driven by passion, you experience an indescribable sense of bliss, a feeling of fulfillment that transcends reality.

Nicki Minaj said, "Something magical happens when you do what you love. Whether it's loved by the masses or not, there's magic in the genuine love you have for your art... and it can never be taken away." Passion is what allowed Criss Angel to persevere through his father's death and nearly two decades of obscurity. This is what he had to say about passion:

"I'm not the most talented person at what I do. I'm not the most talented singer. I'm not the most talented magician. I'm simply more driven than anyone you will ever meet. I'm passionate beyond words. There's nothing that will allow me to fail. And it's because of this attitude that I achieve and live and fulfill my dreams."

The three layers of purpose are the cornerstones of drive and motivation. Through passion, frustration, and/or necessity, you will conquer the three enemies of achievement and skyrocket the process of achieving your goals. **You may refer to the purpose identifier found at www.danmcdaniel.net/action to discover the biggest obstacle to achieving *your* goals and the layer of purpose that will most effectively help you overcome it.**

Now that you know exactly what you want and why you want it, you can begin to discover how to get it. Continue reading onto the next chapter to discover how to build relationships that foster success. In this next chapter, you will learn how to get a mentor who will teach you everything you need to know, gain the praise of influential people (even seemingly "untouchable" celebrities like Oprah Winfrey), and find a support group who will help you achieve your goals. Read on to discover the third step to creating the life you truly want.

Step 3:

Build solid relationships.

"We are the people we interact with. Our paychecks, our moods, the health of our hearts, and the size of our bellies—all of these things are determined by whom we choose to interact with and how."
—Keith Ferrazzi, *Never Eat Alone*

The third step in the process of achieving your goals is building solid relationships. According to world-renowned social psychologist Jonathan Haidt (pronounced "height"), lasting change only occurs when you change your relationships or your environment. Although having a clear vision and a strong purpose are essential, the key to long-term growth and achievement lies within your circle of influence. The people with whom you surround yourself are the single greatest indicator of the direction of your life.

Your core reference group directly determines 1) your mindset 2) your income 3) your health, and 4) your overall level of happiness. Therefore, building solid relationships is the single greatest action step that you can take in order to drastically change your life.

But how do you build new relationships? How do you determine the types of people who should be in your reference group? And, more

19

importantly, how do you approach those people if you think that they would be a good fit? Well, I will answer all of these questions within this chapter. Keep reading to discover how to find a mentor, join a support group, and build the relationships that could forever transform your life.

Change Your Environment

Possibly the most effective strategy for building solid relationships is changing your environment. Your environment, or your surroundings, subconsciously dictates your beliefs, your habits, and your overall mindset as a human being. Therefore, changing your environment (or moving to a different location) may be your best option for creating lasting change and starting your life anew. Some of the world's most notable people cite moving to a different location as the single most defining moment in their lives and/or careers. Had it not been for their decision to change their environment, then a large number of those people could possibly be unknown and insignificant in today's culture. The following are numerous examples of people who thrived after changing their environment.

__*Oprah moved to Chicago.*__ In 1983, then-unknown media proprietor Oprah Winfrey sent an audition tape to Chicago, Illinois, in the hopes of landing the job as host of the local talk show *A.M. Chicago*. After spending seven years as a local television personality in Baltimore, Maryland, Oprah felt the need to change her environment. "I reached a point in Baltimore where I felt I needed to grow myself to the next level," said Winfrey in a 2005 interview.

One of the producers on Oprah's Baltimore-based television show notified her of the job opportunity, and she took action immediately. Oprah stayed up all night with a video editor and sent in her audition tape. Shortly after, she was called for an interview. "As I was flying in to Chicago and walking to State Street to interview for the job, I thought 'I just feel like I belong here.'" Oprah continued, "And if I don't get *this job*, I'm going to figure out how to get *a job* in this city."

Thankfully, she got the job. Oprah began hosting *A.M. Chicago* on January 2, 1984. After only one year as the show's host, *A.M. Chicago* was renamed *The Oprah Winfrey Show*. On September 8, 1986, *The Oprah Winfrey*

Show began its national syndication and dominated the ratings as the number one daytime talk show for 25 years. None of this would have happened if Oprah had not moved to Chicago in 1983.

Jennifer Lopez moved to Hollywood. In 1991, budding entertainer Jennifer Lopez moved to Los Angeles, California, after being casted as a dancer on the 90s hit series *In Living Color.* After two consecutive years on the show, Lopez left to pursue an acting career. As a serious student of her craft, Lopez began taking acting classes. With her newly-acquired skills, Lopez quickly landed her first acting job in 1994 on the Fox series *South Central.* This small role as a "sassy" store clerk opened the doors to various possibilities.

"From that part, both the [production] studio and the network offered me a development deal," said Lopez in a 2014 interview. That development deal led to her landing roles in various other television series. As a young up-and-coming actress, Lopez's experience in television led to her first film role in the 1995 movie *My Family.* Gregory Nava, the director of *My Family,* also casted Lopez in her first leading role in the 1997 film *Selena.* This is the role that launched her into superstardom.

Jennifer Lopez's career came full circle on June 20, 2013, in Los Angeles, California, when she was honored with the 2,500[th] star on the Hollywood Walk of Fame. Director Gregory Nava said the following during the induction ceremony:

> **"When I first met Jennifer, she was a kid from the Bronx. She had never been in a movie. She came [to Hollywood] with no ends and no contacts trying to make it in a town where there were no Latino stars. Nothing came easy for her. She's the hardest worker I have ever known."**

Jennifer Lopez just might possibly be unknown today if it were not for that 1993 relocation from Bronx, New York, to Hollywood, California. Twenty years and over 20 films later, that one decision proved to be the single most defining moment of Jennifer Lopez's career. For this is the result of changing your environment.

Nicki Minaj moved to Atlanta. After becoming dissatisfied with the New York City music scene, rap superstar Nicki Minaj decided to move to the southern epicenter of rap known as Atlanta, Georgia. Feeling inspired by its hip hop culture, Nicki and her longtime companion Safaree (pronounced sŭ-far'-ē) Samuels moved to the bustling city in 2009. Acting completely on faith, she reportedly had only $2,000 to her name.

Reflecting on her relocation in a December 2014 interview with journalist Elliott Wilson, Nicki said, "For a very long time, I didn't even have furniture in Atlanta." Nicki, however, did not allow her lack of financial resources to prevent her relocation. Shortly after moving to Atlanta, Nicki partnered with seasoned star maker Debra Antney and began to thrive in her new environment. She performed at night clubs every week and even recorded her critically acclaimed third mixtape *Beam Me Up Scotty*.

Released on April 18, 2009, this independently released CD helped establish Nicki's fan base and gave her much-needed exposure. The success of this musical album enabled Nicki to sign a multi-million-dollar record deal with Young Money/Universal Records just a few months later. By August 2009, Nicki Minaj's dream of mainstream success had finally come true. However, it is possible that none of this would have happened if Nicki had not changed her environment.

Taylor Swift moved to Nashville. Born into wealth and privilege, Taylor Swift was raised on a 12-acre Christmas tree farm in Reading (pronounced rĕd-ing), Pennsylvania. With two parents in corporate finance, Taylor's family had the financial means and the mental toughness required to help launch Taylor's career into the stratosphere. But before Taylor could dominate the country music charts, she and her family needed to move to Nashville.

Nashville, Tennessee, is widely known as "Music City," the epicenter of country music and the origin of ambition for aspiring musicians worldwide. After watching a television program about country music sensation Faith Hill's rise to superstardom, Taylor discovered that the city of Nashville played a major role in Hill's success. In this moment, Taylor became obsessed with the city and began begging her parents to take her there. Fortunately, Taylor's youthful badgering paid off. At age 11—during a spring vacation from school—Taylor's mother finally took her to Nashville, Tennessee. Unfortunately, however, things didn't quite work out the way they did for Swift's idol Faith Hill.

"When I was 11, I went to Nashville and knocked on the doors of record labels," Swift said. "I walked into every single record label on Music Row. I would run in with my little demo CD and walk up to the receptionist d say, 'Hi, I'm Taylor. I'm 11. I want a record deal. Call me.'" But no one er called. Despite the industry's lack of interest, Taylor decided to persevere. e spent the next three years mastering her craft, learning how to play the itar and writing multiple songs. The next time she went to Nashville, she ould be adequately prepared.

During the summer of 2004—at the tender age of 14—Taylor Swift d her family finally moved to Nashville, Tennessee. It was in this city where aylor performed at Nashville hotspot and songwriters' paradise The Bluebird afé. This music club put singers on the map in Nashville, and Taylor was oking to reserve her spot in the club's rich history. Thankfully, she achieved er goal. While performing on stage, Taylor was spotted by Universal Records ecutive Scott Borchetta. In awe of her performance, Borchetta offered her a cord deal at his upcoming independent label later named Big Machine ecords. Taylor agreed and was signed at age 15.

"I ended up on a record label that let me write every song on my first bum," said Swift. That first album, eponymously titled *Taylor Swift*, was eleased on October 24, 2006, to unexpectedly massive success. Taylor's debut lbum went six times platinum, selling over six million copies worldwide. At nly 16 years old, this was an earth-shattering feat for the young country ausician. The success of this first album led to an international breakthrough rith her second album *Fearless*.

By 2009, Swift had been named Entertainer of the Year by the Country Music Association. In 2010, she won four Grammy Awards, including the award for Album of the Year. This made her the youngest artist ever to gain this distinction. By 2014, she had been twice named Billboard Woman of the Year, signifying leadership and innovation while at the forefront of a booming music career. Ten years after moving to Nashville, Taylor Swift had become a bonafide superstar at the helm of a music revolution. When asked about

Taylor's talent and contribution to the city, country music maven Brad Paisley said the following:

> *__"I would say that, as a songwriter, Taylor is as gifted as a person has ever been who has moved to Nashville... she's become the voice of her generation."__*

Had Taylor Swift and her family not moved to Nashville in 2004, then it is likely that she would not have become "the voice of her generation." Over a decade after moving to "Music City," Taylor Swift now virtually owns the metropolitan. In 2001, she couldn't even get a record deal in the city. In 2013, she performed during a series of sold out shows at the city's famed Bridgestone Arena. With exactly 41,292 screaming fans in attendance, Taylor Swift's *The Red Tour* grossed a reported $3.3 million from September 19–21, 2013, while in Nashville, Tennessee. For this is the result of changing your environment.

__*Tyra Banks moved to Paris.*__ In September 1991, 17-year-old Tyra Banks moved to the fashion capital of the world known as Paris, France. Just three months after graduating from high school, Tyra chose to forego college in pursuit of a modeling career. "My dad had already deposited the check into the account [for my college tuition]," said Tyra in a 2011 interview with E! Entertainment Television. But Tyra gave herself one year to make it as a supermodel. She decided that, if modeling did not work out for her, she would return to school. Tyra reflected on her rationale by saying, "It's a once-in-a-lifetime opportunity, so I'm going to give this Paris thing a try."

Thankfully, everything worked out. Only a few weeks after arriving in Paris, Tyra booked 25 runway shows with the fashion elite, setting a new record for models worldwide. Over the next two years, Tyra travelled all over Europe booking shows in Paris, France; Milan, Italy; and London, England. Hundreds of magazine covers later, she sits atop a fashion and television empire with multiple business entities including the hit series *America's Next Top Model*. None of this would have been possible had it not been for that 1991 move to Paris, France.

**Arnold Schwarzenegger moved to America.** In September 1968, Austrian bodybuilder Arnold Schwarzenegger moved to America. Only 21 years old and speaking with a heavy German accent, Schwarzenegger was determined to make it out of his impoverished home country. "In Austria, kids were conditioned to follow their parents' path. But, unlike the other kids around me, I was very determined to get out of there," said Schwarzenegger in a 2012 interview with ESPN Films. At age 18, Arnold began implementing his plan to leave Austria. While undergoing intensive training during his service in the Austrian Army, Schwarzenegger illegally left his military base to compete in a bodybuilding competition. After winning the competition (and spending one week in solitary confinement), Schwarzenegger gained a new sense of confidence that would later define his unprecedented career.

A few years after leaving the army, Arnold moved to Los Angeles, California, United States, in search of international fame and fortune. "The Mr. Universe title was my ticket to America—the land of opportunity, where I could become a star and get rich," said Schwarzenegger in 2001. Nearly a decade after moving to America, Schwarzenegger retired from bodybuilding and leveraged his new-found fame as five-time Mr. Universe and seven-time Mr. Olympia to land signature movie roles in action films such as _Predator_ and _The Terminator_. After becoming one of the highest-paid actors in Hollywood, Schwarzenegger became "bored" with acting and pursued a career in politics. Arnold Schwarzenegger became the 38th governor of the U.S. state of California in 2003—a remarkable 35 years after emigrating from his home country of Austria. Arnold's success as both an actor and as a governor would not have been possible had he not moved to America in 1968.

When considering changing your environment, ask yourself the following question: **In what culture do I want to immerse myself?** The act of strategically choosing the culture in which to immerse yourself allows you to benefit from both key relationships and the potentially life-changing events that inevitably occur when you are a part of a specific environment. For this is why the aforementioned figures have attained their level of success. Oprah moved to Chicago to expand her opportunities in broadcasting. Jennifer Lopez moved to Hollywood to expand her opportunities in entertainment. Nicki Minaj moved to Atlanta to immerse herself in the city's well-established hip hop culture. Taylor Swift moved to "Music City" to become Nashville's youngest country music star. Tyra Banks moved to Paris to conquer the fashion capital of the world, and Arnold Schwarzenegger moved to America to revolutionize the fitness industry and to dominate the movie market. Decide on the culture in which to immerse yourself, and then proceed to relocate to that region of the world. This just might be the best decision you ever make.

But what if I can't move right now?

If you cannot (or have no desire to) change your environment, then you still have the option of changing your relationships. The quality of your personal relationships is one of the most important factors of your future success. The people with whom you surround yourself determine your rate of growth as well as your standards of achievement. For this is why you must get a mentor and join a mastermind group.

Get a Mentor

The Merriam-Webster Dictionary defines a mentor as, "someone who teaches or gives help and advice to a less experienced and often younger person." Based on this definition, the role of a mentor was designed to help you reach your desired destination by providing a blueprint for you to follow. Finding the right mentor will allow you to avoid common pitfalls and achieve your goals much sooner than you would otherwise.

According to a study of over 100 self-made millionaires, 54% of them had a mentor to help guide them. The other 46% *wished* they had a mentor because they would have become millionaires sooner! Both conducted and published by Jaime Tardy, author of *The Eventual Millionaire*, this study proves that getting an experienced mentor can skyrocket your success. But how do you get a mentor? And, more importantly, how do you find the mentor who is right for you? Well, both of these questions will be answered within the following paragraphs. The most basic principles, however, can be found within this next sentence. When searching for a mentor, ask yourself the following two questions:

1. **Who has already achieved what I want to accomplish?**
2. **How can I help *them*?**

These two questions reveal the fundamentals of both finding the right mentor and approaching him or her in a manner that elicits a positive response. Answering these two questions and utilizing one or more of the following strategies will ensure that you secure a solid mentorship and achieve your goals much sooner than you would otherwise.

Before I tell you the three ways to get a mentor, I must inform you that neither finding nor receiving mentorship is necessarily a formal process. You are not required to become "anointed" as an apprentice in order to benefit from a mentorship. Media strategist Ryan Holiday articulated this concept perfectly when he said, "The mentorships that I've had often started off as very informal and then, based on a mutual exchange of value, grew over time into being something deeper." Based largely on this idea of a mutual exchange of value, let's take a look at the three ways to get a mentor.

3 Ways to Get a Mentor

Throughout my thousands of hours of research for this book, I have found that there are essentially three ways to get a mentor. Regardless of the specific strategy, one central idea remains true: **you must appeal to their self-interest**. When approaching a potential mentor, you must make your offer beneficial to *them*. Your value proposition must be directly related to helping *them* achieve *their* goals or else you carry the risk of being completely ignored. With that being said, here are the three ways to get a mentor.

The first way to get a mentor is to offer free help. When offering free help, you must seek out opportunities in which you are uniquely qualified to add value. This free help, while manifesting in many different forms, often leads to unforeseen opportunities. When asked about the main communication technique he used to network with influencers (before he attained worldwide acclaim), rock star bestselling author and investor Tim Ferriss attributed his early connections to volunteering. When Tim arrived in Silicon Valley in his early twenties, he had no connections and very little money. In fact, Tim recalls driving a "hand-me-down" minivan with no back seats! Embarrassed and desperate to build new relationships, Tim volunteered for a non-profit startup.

"I was starting from ground zero—just like everybody does." Tim continued, "I worked at the front desk. I did *way* more than I was asked to do. And, as a result, I was viewed as more responsible; therefore, I became more important to the organization." After a few months as a dedicated volunteer, Tim was given the opportunity to run a major event. This gave him the authority to choose a panel of speakers and to invite all of the people he had dreamed of meeting. One of those people was Jack Canfield, co-author of *The Success Principles* and co-creator of the *Chicken Soup for the Soul* series of bestselling books.

Because of his newly-formed relationship with the book marketing maven, Jack introduced Tim to the veteran book agent who sold Tim's mega-bestseller-turned-international phenomenon called *The 4-Hour Workweek* to New York City publishing executives. Had Tim Ferriss not volunteered for that non-profit startup and built a personal relationship with author Jack Canfield, it is possible that the "4-hour phenomenon" would have never existed.

Although volunteering has been shown to generate positive results, it is not the only way to effectively offer free help. Sometimes, a simple email can get you into the network of a top achiever. Let's take a look at how Charlie Hoehn (pronounced hōn) got Tim Ferriss to be his mentor shortly after the "4-hour phenomenon."

Case Study: Charlie Hoehn

After graduating college during a recession, Charlie Hoehn had trouble finding a job. He was reportedly rejected by multiple companies, including a company with which he had completed an internship. After months of disappointment, Charlie decided to try a different approach. Instead of sending his resume to companies (like every other college graduate), Charlie decided to offer free work to some of his biggest role models. One of those people was Tim Ferriss.

In his book *Recession-Proof Graduate: How to Land the Job You Want by Doing Free Work*, Charlie recommends researching your target mentor and reaching out to them. This is the exact strategy that Charlie used to gain Tim Ferriss as a mentor. He leveraged a relationship with Ramit Sethi (pronounced rŭ-mēt → say-tē), a friend of Tim's, to gain an email introduction. To read the full email, go to **www.danmcdaniel.net/email**.

> <u>Note:</u> I would strongly recommend that you temporarily bookmark this page and go read this email in its entirety. It gives context to the remaining paragraphs of this case study and serves as a world-class blueprint for emailing influencers.

Within this email, Charlie immediately explains how he will help Tim. Charlie offered Tim free video production services in exchange for a mentorship. By mentioning that he has "been editing video for more than four years," Charlie proves that he is not just some random guy out in cyberspace. By stating that "this video will establish an even deeper credibility with your new (and old) readers," Charlie explains how his expertise can specifically benefit Tim's business.

At the end of the email, Charlie perfectly describes the role of a mentor when he explains to Tim how this mentorship would benefit him as the provider of the service. Charlie so eloquently describes everything I have been trying to teach you in this chapter when he wrote the following: "...**you've already done what I want to become:** an entrepreneur who travels a lot. Working with you would allow me to really mentally shift gears and help <u>move me towards my goals faster.</u>"

Just one year after sending this email, Charlie Hoehn went on a nationwide 31-city movie tour with mega-bestselling author and connoisseur of controversy Tucker Max. He went on to write several popular books of his own and has led multiple workshops as a professional speaker. After being featured in major publications such as *Forbes*, *Harvard Business Review*, and CBS

News, Charlie has established himself as a trusted marketing consultant and video production specialist. As a result of the experiences he gained with Tim Ferriss, Charlie Hoehn has finally achieved his goal: he is "an entrepreneur who travels a lot." For this is the result of offering free help.

Sometimes, an offer for free help can unexpectedly turn into a paid apprenticeship. Let's take a look at how media strategist Ryan Holiday transitioned his offer for free help into the opportunity of a lifetime—a paid apprenticeship with bestselling author Robert Greene.

Case Study: Ryan Holiday

"I learned how to create books from Robert. Robert taught me how to research books. He showed me how a book is built."
—Ryan Holiday

As an aspiring author, young journalist-turned-media strategist Ryan Holiday began his career as a writer for his college newspaper. Always ambitious and constantly seeking out rather obscure opportunities, Ryan leveraged his position to interview some of the people he admired. One of those people was bestselling author Tucker Max. After writing a news article about him, Ryan approached Tucker with an offer to work for free. Ryan, who kept up with Tucker's recent activities, offered to help Tucker resolve a few online marketing issues that were negatively affecting his business. When reflecting on this approach in a 2014 interview on London Real, Ryan said, "I really wanted to be a writer, and I wanted to be around other writers. But I was 19 years old, and I felt like I had nothing to contribute." Ryan continued, "But I *did* understand how the Internet worked…"

After helping Tucker with that initial project, Ryan had gained his trust and was given more responsibility. By the end of his sophomore year in college, Ryan had moved into Tucker's home and began working as an intern for his media company that helped authors build a brand online. "I was sleeping on Tucker's floor," Ryan said. "We lived in this crappy house in the ghetto of Los Angeles." Because Ryan was producing exceptional work for

Tucker's company, Tucker invited Ryan to lunch with him and his friend Robert Greene. Young Ryan Holiday had no idea that this luncheon would change his life forever.

During the luncheon, Robert Greene mentioned that he was working on a book with rapper 50 Cent and needed a research assistant. Using every ounce of his willpower to mask his author-worshipping enthusiasm, Ryan virtually leaped at the opportunity. "I was a huge Robert Greene fan," Ryan said. "I had read all of his books." Refusing to let Ryan work for free, Robert paid him to be his research assistant. As a requirement for the job, Ryan learned Robert's note-taking system and performed various menial tasks. Some of those tasks included reading lengthy historical texts and painstakingly transcribing interviews.

Maintaining a positive attitude while performing these somewhat mundane tasks, Ryan felt like he had hit the lottery when he was allowed to sit in on a conversation between book publishing maven Robert Greene and multi-millionaire hip hop mogul 50 Cent. As the person responsible for recording and transcribing this interview, Ryan realized that he had landed the opportunity of a lifetime. The book that Ryan helped Robert Greene develop was titled *The 50th Law* and became a *New York Times* best seller in 2009. Ryan was credited in the acknowledgements.

When asked what he had learned from Robert Greene, Ryan replied, "I learned how to create books from Robert. Robert taught me how to research books. He showed me how a book is built." Ryan continued by stating that he learned the most simply by being in Robert's presence and by observing his dedication to the craft of writing. By the end of the summer after his sophomore year, Ryan had dropped out of college to pursue other opportunities. Now out of Tucker's home and into his own apartment, Ryan simultaneously worked for Robert Greene, Tucker Max, and a talent management company in Hollywood over the next several years. But Ryan's story doesn't end there.

Because his mentor Robert Greene was on the Board of Directors at American Apparel, Robert introduced Ryan to then-CEO Dov (pronounced dŭv) Charney. This introduction led to Ryan becoming Director of Marketing at American Apparel at age 21. Introduction after introduction, Ryan slowly became a modern-day marketing maven and trusted media strategist for some of the largest, most notable corporations in the world. Now a rather prolific mega-bestselling author in his own right, Ryan largely credits his success to those early mentorships. With books published in over a dozen languages (before his 30th birthday), Ryan Holiday has proven that becoming an apprentice may be one of the best decisions that you ever make.

The second way to get a mentor is to become a client. When you become the client of a mentor, you are providing monetary value to him or her in the form of direct payment. This direct payment may occur in a number of ways, including but not limited to: the purchase of a product, the attending of an event, and the receiving of consulting. Regardless of the modality, becoming a client is one of the best ways to get a mentor. Let's take a look at how Internet radio show host John Lee Dumas directly benefited from becoming the client of online broadcasting extraordinaire Jaime Tardy.

Case Study: John Lee Dumas

During the summer of 2012, U.S. Army officer-turned-law school dropout John Lee Dumas wanted a change. After working for several years in both corporate finance and commercial real estate, John had grown tired of the daily grind. He had become fed up with his cozy corporate conundrum of 12-hour workdays and constant career changes. In search of a more meaningful existence (and, perhaps, a few business ideas), John began listening to podcasts during his daily commute. These Internet radio shows inspired John to create his own show, so he reached out to veteran podcaster Jaime Tardy for guidance.

After reading John's heartfelt email about his vision for a daily podcast, Jaime agreed to meet him in person. They were both residents of Maine, so this made scheduling an in-person consultation fairly simple. John drove an hour to meet Jaime at the Starbucks coffee shop closest to her home; and, after a stellar meeting, he immediately became a client. John began paying Jaime $1,000 per month for one-on-one coaching. During the first three months of his journey as a podcaster, John had a veteran online radio show host to walk him through the entire process. This guidance proved to be invaluable, as it allowed John to avoid the often inevitable pitfalls that come with launching an online show.

"I was clueless about podcasting," said John. Thankfully, this apparent "cluelessness" wasn't very noticeable, as John had an all-star lineup of guests for the launch of his new show. He attained this list of highly-sought-after guests as a result of his mentorship with Jaime Tardy. Shortly after becoming a client, Jaime took John to a New York City business conference at which she was a keynote speaker. At this conference, Jaime introduced John to key influencers within their industry.

"I got to know [key influencers] for the very first time in a face-to-face setting," said John. It was during this conference when John asked these influencers to be featured guests on his upcoming podcast. This series of introductions led to John conducting over 40 different interviews with entrepreneurs before he even launched his daily show! It would have been nearly impossible for John to connect with this many high achievers in such a short period of time without the influence of his mentor Jaime Tardy.

Even though John had recorded over three dozen interviews for his upcoming show, he was still afraid to launch. Feelings of inferiority started to creep into John's psyche, and he began to feel as though he were not qualified enough to host a show. "I have no experience in podcasting," thought John. "Why should people listen to *me*?" These thoughts further paralyzed John with fear, prompting him to delay the launch of his podcast by five weeks. Growing increasingly frustrated by John's excuses for not yet launching his show, Jaime threatened to fire *him* as a client. "The fear of losing Jaime as a mentor was much stronger than [the fear of] failing as a podcaster," said John. Jaime's ultimatum led to the immediate launch of his online show.

In September 2012, John Lee Dumas finally launched his podcast Entrepreneur on Fire. Within the next year, John's show consistently rose up the iTunes charts as it was being downloaded by millions of people worldwide. By the summer of 2013, he was making money, changing lives, and networking with the business elite. Entrepreneur on Fire was a massive success that gained momentum fairly quickly because John had a five-star mentor. But the story doesn't end there. After celebrating the one-year anniversary of his show, John decided to hire another mentor: online marketing maven Lewis Howes. A former professional athlete-turned-online business extraordinaire, Lewis Howes made a fortune by hosting online seminars, or webinars, and selling educational products over the Internet. John had heard the news, and he wanted a similar result; therefore, in September 2013, John hired Lewis as a mentor.

After three months of solid coaching, **John's net income had exceeded $100,000 per month**. This was the direct result of strategic advertising as well as marketing fundamentals that John had learned from Lewis. By April 2014—only seven months after hiring Lewis—John's company generated over $200,000 in a single month! Take a look at Entrepreneur on Fire's meteoric growth:

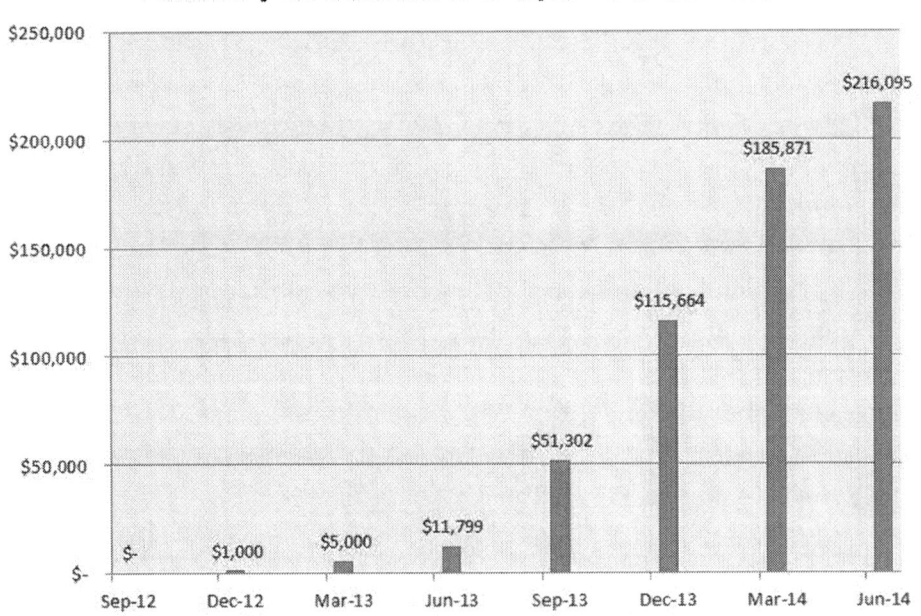

After just over 18 months in business, Entrepreneur on Fire had far exceeded even John's original mentor's expectations. With fewer than three employees, John and his life and business partner Kate had taken the podcasting industry by storm. They got to avoid amateur mistakes and speed past potential pitfalls because they hired the right people. After less than two years in business, John reportedly had a net worth that far exceeded $2 million. He and Kate receive letters of appreciation from show listeners in every part of the world every single day of the week. For these are the results of hiring the right mentor(s).

The third way to get a mentor is to provide a testimonial. Providing a testimonial is possibly **the most powerful technique for building relationships with mentors**. When you provide a testimonial, you are informing a potential mentor of how they have *already* changed your life. You are essentially describing how their information, their product, and/or their service has created positive (and tangible) results in your own life and/or business. Your job as the provider of a testimonial is to communicate personal transformation.

When you communicate this transformation, your potential mentor will relish in egoic pride and share your story with the world. Providing a results-based testimonial is the surefire way of getting into the heart and into the mind of a mentor and potentially staying there forever. Let's take a look at how I leveraged a testimonial to connect with world-renowned fitness icon and World Wrestling Entertainment, Inc. (WWE) Hall of Famer Trish Stratus.

"I lost 90 pounds using your program…"

On April 26, 2008, Canadian entrepreneur and fitness guru Trish Stratus opened Canada's largest eco-friendly yoga studio Stratusphere Yoga. At this time, I measured 5 feet 11 inches tall and weighed 240 pounds. According to the body mass index (BMI) calculator provided by the U.S. Department of Health and Human Services, I was categorized as "obese." Frustrated and uniquely positioned for a future of self-inflicted (and potentially life-threatening) health problems, I knew that it was time for a change. Inspired by the opening of Stratusphere, I began to practice yoga. By 2010—after two years of consistent progress—I had lost 90 pounds. Holy cannoli! I couldn't believe it…

Transformed and incredibly thankful, I decided to express my appreciation. It was only because Trish Stratus—someone whose business acumen I admired—had introduced me to yoga that I decided to give it a try. So when she released her first yoga DVD, I was one of her biggest ambassadors. In fact, I flew 1,300 miles across the country to demonstrate my support!

On October 29, 2011—after taking a 5-hour flight from Baton Rouge, Louisiana, to Langhorne, Pennsylvania—I met Trish Stratus during her U.S. promotional tour for Stratusphere Yoga. The experience is best described in the following excerpt from my first book *Extreme Honesty*:

"Finally, the moment had come. Trish Stratus was standing right in front of me. My heart was pounding with anticipation. I was next in line—ticket-holder number six. I took a deep breath and walked toward her smiling face. I told Trish where I was from and how she and yoga had changed my life. Quickly, she arose from her seat and gave me a big warm hug. (I was the first fan to receive such a greeting.) We talked for what literally ended up being a 10-minute-long conversation—un-heard-of at an autograph signing! She was genuinely interested in my story and was tremendously humbled that I had traveled so far. Due to the quality of our extended meeting, Trish promised that we would chat after the signing.

After the signing, when all other fans had departed, Trish decided that she wanted to document my story. As promised, she pulled out her personal cell phone and recorded the two of us on camera. She expressed how proud she was of my 90-pound weight loss and promised to upload the video. My life was now complete."

> __Note:__ To watch this exclusive video, please visit **www.danmcdaniel.net/stratusphere**.

As a result of providing this testimonial, I got to connect with one of my personal heroines by helping her achieve *her* goal of getting the entire world to do yoga. Wow! What a full-circle moment. This moment also led to other opportunities. Largely due to Trish's widespread media coverage, several journalists also became interested in my story. Within the next few days, I was featured in the Canadian publication *Toro Magazine* as well as on the international television network CNBC. For these are the results of providing a testimonial.

> **Note:** To watch my feature on CNBC, please visit **www.danmcdaniel.net/cnbc**.

If you don't quite have the resources (or the desire) to fly one thousand miles across the country to provide a testimonial, then you can always communicate your transformation via phone, physical mail, electronic mail, or through one of the countless other modern-day outlets at your disposal. The key is to deliver your message in the modality that best serves your target influencer. A person like Trish Stratus would have been nearly impossible to connect with through email. In person, however, I was given unprecedented access. You must communicate in the form that best serves your recipient.

It must also be noted that, in the aforementioned example, I did not expect to obtain such extraordinary results. I simply wanted to express my gratitude to Trish for legitimately changing my life. It was only in retrospect that I understood that providing a testimonial was a world-class networking strategy. Please use this strategy with integrity.

The three ways to get a mentor are as follows: offer free help, become a client, or provide a testimonial. Each of these three strategies—when used as described above—will almost guarantee a positive response and will begin a mutually beneficial relationship with a potential mentor. The next best strategy for building solid relationships is to join a mastermind group.

Join a Mastermind Group

Made popular by the 1937 self-help classic *Think and Grow Rich* by Napoleon Hill, a mastermind is a group of people strategically assembled in the pursuit of a common goal. Whether paid or unpaid, a mastermind group is an exclusive community of achievers who meet regularly to share knowledge, seek guidance, gain support, and provide accountability. These regular meetings may consist of either small groups or large groups and may occur in person, over the phone, or by other technological means such as video chat. Depending on its structure, a mastermind group may assemble either daily, weekly, monthly, or quarterly. Its number of members may range from only three people to two hundred people or more. A mastermind's structure is based solely on the preference of its participants. To better understand what a mastermind group is and how one actually works, take a look at the three most common structures of a mastermind group.

Mastermind A

Location: San Diego, California, United States
Number of Participants: 3-5
Target Demographic: Men aged 18-25
Common Goal/Purpose: To improve dating life
Frequency of Assembly: Weekly
Price: FREE

Mastermind B

Location: World Wide Web
Number of Participants: 100
Target Demographic: Nonfiction self-help authors
Common Goal/Purpose: To sell more books
Frequency of Assembly: Bi-weekly
Price: $75 per month

Mastermind C

Location: Necker Island
Number of Participants: 25
Target Demographic: Wealthy businesspeople
Common Goal/Purpose: To increase annual revenue
Frequency of Assembly: Quarterly
Price: $25,000 per year

In Mastermind A, a small group of young men meet at a local coffee shop every Sunday night. With the common goal of improving their dating life, these young men openly discuss their individual challenges in regards to meeting compatible women. Although the members of this group individually present their problems, they collectively provide solutions. This mastermind group requires no membership fee and is somewhat informal in its structure.

In Mastermind B, a group of writers (most of whom have never met in person) gather together every other week to attend video conference calls that help them sell more books. With access to a private forum, members have the opportunity to give and receive feedback on book ideas, recommend top-rated editors, and share insider knowledge about the publishing industry. This mastermind group costs $75 per month to join.

In Mastermind C, a group of wealthy businesspeople gather together on a private island every three months to discuss revenue generation. Because these businesspeople are incredibly busy, organizing a weekly (or even a monthly) meeting would be nearly impossible to schedule. Each businessperson in the group owns a multi-million-dollar company; therefore, the ideas presented during these meetings are literally worth millions! The $25,000-per-year price point is well worth the investment when the business owner doubles or quadruples his revenue as a direct result of the insights and the relationships gained from joining the mastermind.

Let's take a look at how socially-conscious entrepreneur and personal growth pioneer Vishen Lakhiani (pronounced vish'-in → lock'-ē-annie) quadrupled his business as a result of joining a few mastermind groups.

Case Study: Vishen Lakhiani

Vishen Lakhiani is the founder of Mindvalley, a multi-million-dollar personal growth publishing company that sells educational products over the Internet. Starting the company in 2003 with just $700 and a laptop, Vishen struggled to stay afloat in the high-rent district of Lower Manhattan, New York. In fact, his first five years in business were tumultuous. By May 2008, Vishen's company Mindvalley was losing $15,000 per month and on the verge of a massive layoff. Frustrated with his failing company, Vishen decided to stop trying to build a business by himself. He decided to finally invest in relationships. "I got on a plane and started attending masterminds," Vishen said. He continued:

"I found mentors—some of whom I paid $2,500 per hour. I traveled to meet smart people I respected and took them out to lunch. I attended seminars, networked, formed tribes and 'learning groups,' and soaked up all of the knowledge I received. I stopped trying to do it solo—and, instead, sought to connect with other bright minds and learn from them."

Some of these "bright minds" included business titans Tony Robbins, Richard Branson, and Steve Forbes (editor-in-chief of *Forbes* business magazine). Vishen received counsel from success coach Tony Robbins in Fiji, and he connected with billionaire businessman Richard Branson in the British Virgin Islands. As a result of the advice he received from these seasoned entrepreneurs, Vishen and his team had doubled Mindvalley's total revenue by 2009—just one year after facing financial turmoil. In 2008, Mindvalley reportedly generated less than $5 million in revenue, losing approximately $15,000 per month. The company was making money; however, it was <u>not</u> profitable. Its expenses exceeded its revenue.

By 2009—after receiving coaching—Mindvalley generated nearly $10 million and finally become a profitable business. By 2012, Mindvalley had 200 employees in dozens of countries around the globe. That year, the company reportedly generated nearly $20 million. This means that **Mindvalley increased its annual revenue by 400% in just four years** as a result of its founder attending masterminds! Take a look at the graph on the following page for a visual representation of the company's meteoric growth:

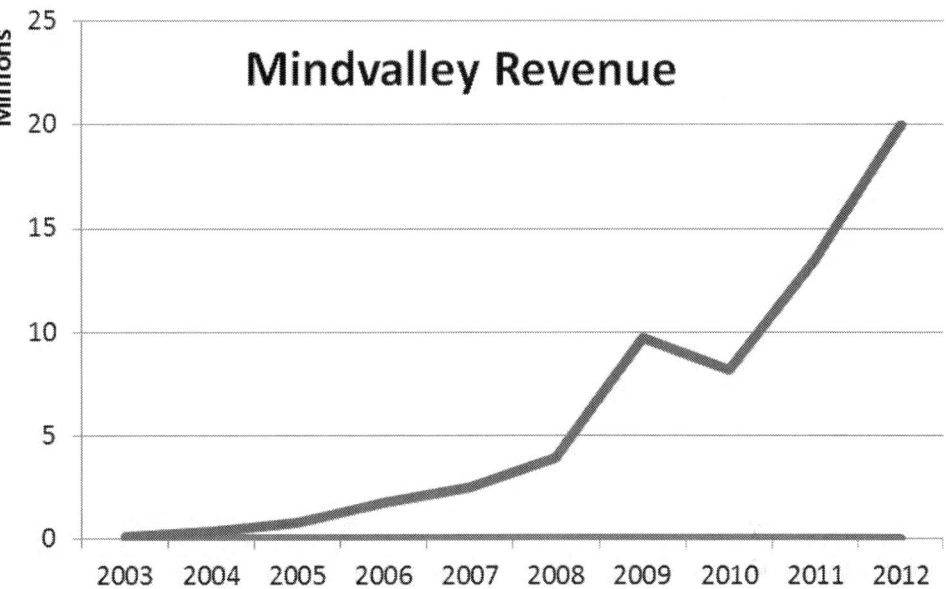

This explosion of income allows Mindvalley to regularly donate hundreds of thousands of dollars to charity. In fact, the company reportedly donates 100% of the proceeds from its flagship event Awesomeness Fest to various causes and organizations that promote social reform and global education. Vishen Lakhiani, through his company Mindvalley, gets to make money *and* positively impact the world. For this is the power of joining a mastermind group.

Now that you know the benefits of joining a mastermind group, you must now find the group that is right for you. When searching for a mastermind group, you must ensure that its members have goals that are similar to those that you have established for yourself. Consider both its structure and its meeting frequency before deciding to commit to a group.

Get an Accountability Partner

One of the best benefits of joining a mastermind group is the fact that you can get an accountability partner. Regardless of the number of people in your mastermind group, having at least one person to hold you accountable will dramatically increase your chances of achieving your goals. The right accountability partner will help you cut through the B.S. and blast past procrastination. He or she will add massive value to your life and you will add an equal amount of value to his or her life. The mutual exchange of accountability is what makes the partnership work.

I personally have four accountability partners—Daniel, Austin, Saad (pronounced Sŏd), and Randy—all of whom I met through a mastermind group. I hold Daniel accountable as he writes and performs original music while building his career as a recording artist. I hold Austin accountable as he increases his fitness, improves his relationships, and builds a personal growth company from scratch. I hold Saad accountable by monitoring his daily caloric intake as he progresses toward his goal of losing weight. I also hold Randy accountable as he successfully builds his real estate portfolio. They each hold *me* accountable as I consistently create products and build an online publishing empire. When one of us fails to meet a weekly milestone, there are consequences to our lack of action. In fact, I once paid Randy $100 because I failed to complete a chapter of this very book within the proposed timeline! Continue reading for the full story.

"I'm still on chapter one…"

I began drafting *The Ultimate Guide to Success* in early January 2015. By mid-February 2015, I was *still* writing Chapter 1. In other words, it took me nearly six weeks to both write and type only 3,000 words! That's ridiculous. In my defense, I was working 40+ hours per week at my day job *and* working through paperback formatting complications; however, these were not the only issues. The truth is… *I procrastinated.* I procrastinated and I resisted the actual act of writing because I was afraid. Afraid of doing the one thing that I was born to do. And Randy knew it.

Randy also knew that I had previously written full-length books for clients in four weeks or less (before I got the new job). Because of this, Randy said to me, "Dan, you need to treat yourself like your highest-paying client." This meant that I needed to cut the crap and complete my writing on schedule. When I was working with elite clients, I always completed their projects by our scheduled deadline—mainly because we had a contract in place and because they were *paying me* for my services. This knowing sparked an epiphany.

In the effort to associate pain with procrastination, I drafted a contract with a very interesting "consequence" clause: the person who fails to achieve his goal within the proposed timeline must pay his partner $50. After failing to complete Chapter 1 (the second time!), I paid Randy $50. After failing to complete Chapter 2 by my intended deadline, I paid him another $50. After paying Randy $100 in one month (for procrastination), I had finally learned my lesson. If you are reading this book right now, then our partnership has proven beneficial.

> **Note:** To download the accountability agreement, go to **www.danmcdaniel.net/action**.

As proven through the various case studies in this chapter, you can begin to transform your life by building solid relationships. Simply change your environment, get a mentor, and join a mastermind group. Regardless of the means, get an accountability partner to help you blast past procrastination and push through feelings of inferiority. Establish these relationships and watch your life soar! Continue reading to discover how to establish empowering beliefs and train your mind to subconsciously create the life you want.

Step 4:

Establish empowering beliefs.

"You become what you believe."
—Oprah Winfrey

The fourth step in the process of achieving your goals is establishing empowering beliefs. Before you can begin living the life you want, you must identify the thoughts, the stories, and the behaviors that are holding you back. These false ideas about who you are and what you are capable of have been woven deep into your subconscious as a result of several years (or maybe even several *decades*) of conditioning. This psychological training, most of which has gone unnoticed by you, is the reason for your current beliefs and is largely the cause of your present-day circumstances. Essentially, **the life you lead is the result of what you have been trained to believe**.

But who has engrained these beliefs into your psyche? If not you, then who or what is responsible for the thoughts and the ideas instilled within your mind about who you are and, even more importantly, who you are capable of becoming? Well, all of these answers can be found by reviewing your history. Certain <u>events</u>, certain <u>individuals</u>, and even certain <u>environments</u> from your past (and possibly even from your *present*) have all contributed to your beliefs.

Parenting, school, work, relationships, and popular culture are some of the factors that have significantly impacted your world view as well as your subconscious beliefs. This accumulation of experiences has resulted in the life you currently live.

But how do you examine these past experiences? How do you determine the specific consequences that have resulted from your internal beliefs? Well, the answer is simple: you must identify your *interpretation* of past events. In other words, you must determine what a certain event *really means* to you by examining how your new level of understanding has affected your decision-making process in past situations. For a better understanding of this principle, take a look at the following examples:

CAREER	
Event	You are told your entire life (by parents, by teachers, and by commercial media) that success and security result from a college education and a "steady" corporate job.
Interpretation	**"Following the traditional path will make me happy and fulfilled."**
Result	You settle for a career, a marriage, a mortgage, and a life that you ultimately hate.

LOVE	
Event	A guy (or a girl) breaks your heart in high school.
Interpretation	**"Falling in love leads to pain and heartache."**
Result	You end up lonely and depressed, finding it nearly impossible to trust anyone or to be vulnerable, even though love is the one thing that you really want.

• •

MONEY	
Event	While growing up, your parents constantly argued about money. They often stated that, "Money doesn't grow on trees."
Interpretation	**"Money is a source of stress. Money is also a scarce resource, incredibly difficult to acquire."**
Result	You are constantly stressed out about money, working 12-15 hours per day, still just *barely* making enough money to survive.

In Example A, a man settles for a life that he despises simply because he thought that was what he was *supposed to do*. In Example B, a woman deprives herself of intimacy simply because *one guy* (over a decade ago!) betrayed her trust. In Example C, a man unconsciously chooses a life of poverty because his parents conditioned him for scarcity. **Your entire life can be dictated by your *interpretation* of a single event if you do not carefully examine your past experiences**. But how can you prevent the potential pain and agony often associated with internalized beliefs? How do you move forward with power and conviction when you hold the beliefs of a corrupt and unfortunate history? Well, both of these questions will be answered within the next few paragraphs.

Change Your Story

The way to establish empowering beliefs (even with a history of negative experiences) is to change your story. When you change your story, or the beliefs that you have about who you are and what you are capable of, you are in the position to radically change your life. Your story is simply a script in your mind that dictates your behavior. It is developed through a series of past events and is reinforced by repeated results. In order to change this internal script, you must affirm your intentions for the future. Let's take a look at how rock star financial advisor Suze Orman (pronounced Susie → or'-men) transformed her poverty-stricken beliefs into abundant intentions to become one of the highest-paid financial professionals in the world.

Case Study: Suze Orman

"I was paralyzed with fear, so I decided to create a new truth."
—Suze Orman

Growing up in the crime-ridden neighborhood of South Side, Chicago, Illinois, Suze Orman never dreamed that she would someday become the world's most trusted financial advisor. With a mother who worked as a secretary and a father who was frequently ill, Suze's childhood reflected the exact opposite of financial abundance. "My parents had no money," said Suze in a 2015 interview at AOL Headquarters. "I was never expected to be anybody or [to achieve] anything," continued Suze. In alignment with the low expectations thrusted upon her, Suze moved to California in her early twenties to land her "dream job" as a waitress. "I remained a waitress until I was [almost] 30 years of age, making $400 per month," said Suze.

After seven years as a waitress, Suze decided to pursue greater ambitions. Because she was behind on a few personal loans, Suze sought to get a better-paying job in order to pay back her creditors. Suze then took advantage of the early 1980s affirmative action laws and landed a job as a stockbroker. "They hired me to fill their women's quota," said Suze in a 2012 interview with the Archive of American Television. In the wake of good fortune, Suze became the only female stockbroker at the prestigious Oakland, California, financial services firm Merrill Lynch. Here, she began making $1,500 per month—almost four times her previous salary as a waitress! However, with this surge in income came a surge of disempowering beliefs.

"I knew I didn't belong there. I was a waitress," said Suze. While most of the other financial advisors at Merrill Lynch drove luxury cars such as Mercedes-Benzes and BMWs, Suze reportedly drove a 1967 Volvo Station Wagon. She often recalls how her colleagues would eat lunch at high-end restaurants while she ate lunch at Taco Bell! To combat her insecurities, Suze decided to create a new truth. Her new truth was as follows: **"I am young, powerful, and successful, producing at least $10,000 per month."** Suze reportedly affirmed this new truth—whether through written form or through spoken form—at least 25 times per day.

"Every time I got afraid, I recited that truth," said Suze. She continued, "Within six months, that truth became a reality." Now victorious against her lack of confidence in this new profession, Suze had finally conquered her fear of inadequacy as a budding financial advisor. As a result of changing her story, she went from a struggling waitress making $400 per month to a thriving financial professional producing over $10,000 per month. Nearly 35 years later, Suze said, "There are times now when I can make $10,000 *per minute*." Wow! For this is the result of changing your story.

As you have learned from the aforementioned case study, changing your story can also dramatically change your life. It allows you to go from a limiting state of mind to a limitless state of reality. But what happens if you don't know your story? What do you do if you are unaware of the thoughts and the ideas that are holding you back? Well, the answer is simple. Continue reading to discover how to uncover your hidden beliefs.

Uncover Your Hidden Beliefs

The key to changing your story and to ultimately transforming your life lies in your ability to uncover your hidden beliefs. Hidden beliefs lie deep within your psyche, underneath years (or even decades) of conditioning, functioning as agents of your subconscious and architects of your destiny. The fastest, most effective way to uncover these hidden beliefs is to answer the following question: **why haven't I achieved my goal already?** Your *honest* answer to this question will reveal all of your excuses, your limiting beliefs, and even your negative conditioning. Some of the most common answers to this question are as follows:

- **"I'm too old."**
- **"I'm too young."**
- **"I don't have any credentials and/or qualifications."**
- **"I don't have enough time."**
- **"I don't have enough money."**

The answer is, sometimes, very easy to diagnose. Other times, however, the answer speaks to the very core of the human experience. Oftentimes, the answer is expressed in some form of the phrase, "I'm not good enough." You may feel as if you are, for some reason, unworthy of the life that you were born to live. Your subconscious constantly echoes the question, "Who am I to be successful?" But the real question is, "Who am I *not* to be?" You were created to complete a distinct personal mission, to fulfill a supreme personal destiny that was uniquely appointed to you; therefore, it is eternally prohibited for you to allow a set of corrupt beliefs to impede your mission. Use the following five-step process to blast past your limiting beliefs and fulfill your unique personal destiny.

Step 1: **Answer the following question: why haven't I achieved my goal already?** As previously discussed, your answer to this question will reveal all of your excuses, your limiting beliefs, and your negative conditioning.

Step 2: **State your limiting belief. This step allows you to clearly identify the thoughts and the ideas that are preventing you from achieving your goals.**

Step 3: **Turn it around.** This step allows you to turn your limiting belief into an empowering belief.

Step 4: **Affirm your new belief.** Repeat your new belief until you have re-programmed your mind for success.

Step 5: **Commit to its achievement.** Use the strategies in the next chapter to take action on your new beliefs.

In the effort to help you better understand how to implement this strategy, I will use the aforementioned case study of financial advisor Suze Orman to illustrate these five steps.

Step 1: **Answer the following question: why haven't I achieved my goal already?**

Step 2: **State your limiting belief** (the answer from Step 1).

"I don't belong here. I'm just a waitress."

Step 3: **Turn it around.** "I am young, powerful, and successful, producing at least $10,000 per month."

Step 4: **Affirm your new belief.** Suze reportedly either wrote or spoke her new belief at least 25 times per day.

Step 5: **Commit to its achievement.** Suze not only affirmed her intentions, but she also worked tirelessly to reach this career milestone within six months of setting her goal.

The key to establishing empowering beliefs is to affirm a mental script that is simultaneously short, unrestrictive, and foretelling of your future success. Notice that Suze's new belief affirmed that she would be "producing *at least* $10,000 per month." It was fairly short—only one sentence—so that she could easily recite it. Her empowering belief is the exact opposite of her limiting belief, and she structured it as if it had already happened. For these are the elements of a truly empowering belief. **You may refer to the state-of-the-art limiting beliefs eliminator found at <u>www.danmcdaniel.net/action</u> to further establish your own set of empowering beliefs.** Otherwise, continue reading to discover how to turn your new set of beliefs into an action plan of achievement.

Step 5:

Take immediate action.

"When you are not pursuing your goal, you are literally committing spiritual suicide."
—Les Brown

The fifth step in the process of achieving your goals is taking immediate action. When you take *immediate* action, you temporarily eradicate all feelings of inferiority and move (with seemingly superhuman capabilities) toward your ultimate destination. World-renowned motivational speaker Les Brown believes that chronically neglecting your goals ultimately leads to "spiritual suicide," the feeling that a part of you will *die* if you do not at least *try* to achieve a specific goal. **Spiritual suicide is the feeling of your soul suffering, your cowardice rumbling, and your faith crumbling in the ashes of your shattered dreams.**

It is the feeling of being physically alive yet spiritually extinct. The worst part, though, is that this is all by your own design. (It *is* called spiritual "suicide," after all.) Because you are responsible for the death of your spirit, you are also responsible for the revival of your soul. Take heed to your aspirations. For immediate action will bring you back to life.

Not only can action renew your spirit, but it can also lead to life-changing opportunities. Let's take a look at how rapper Big Sean took immediate action and landed a record deal with music mogul Kanye West.

Case Study: Big Sean

Born Sean Anderson, Detroit, Michigan, rapper Big Sean received the opportunity of a lifetime one Saturday morning during the summer of 2005. Only 17 years of age—just a few weeks before beginning his senior year of high school—Sean received the phone call that would forever shape his destiny. Unbeknownst to him, hip hop titan (and one of his biggest inspirations) Kanye West was making an appearance at the local radio station 102.7 FM to promote his second album *Late Registration*. Upon hearing the news, Sean's friend Tony Zuko contacted him immediately. It was this phone call that would forever change Sean Anderson's life.

While in line at a local bank to cash his $100 check from his job as a telemarketer, Sean received a call from his friend Tony encouraging him to drive down to the radio station and rap for Kanye West. "The idea was so inspiring that I dropped everything I was doing. I didn't [even] cash the check," said Sean in a 2011 interview. In a frantic rush, he then grabbed one of his CDs, borrowed gas money from a friend, and drove down the highway to 102.7 FM. Because he performed at the radio station every Friday night, Sean got through Radio One security without hassle.

"I looked down the hall and saw [Kanye West] and his entourage just standing there in the radio station," said Sean. Evidently, Kanye's segment had just concluded. In a hurry to get to his next location while promoting his newly-released album, Kanye and his entourage began walking out of the station. In awe of his hero and recognizing this once-in-a-lifetime opportunity, Sean virtually begged Kanye to allow him to demonstrate his skills. Initially reluctant, Kanye gave Sean permission to rap for him as he walked out of the building. "I was rapping for, like, ten minutes straight," said Sean.

Positively reacting to punch lines and giving Sean the rapper's head nod of approval, Kanye West obviously liked what he heard. Captivated by Sean's freestyle flow and lucid lyricism, Kanye West accepted his CD and logged his contact information. For this was the beginning of something magical. That magic, however, took quite some time to take form. The next two years of Sean's life was marred by struggle, sacrifice, and uncertainty.

"I gave up a scholarship to [Michigan State University]," said Sean. "I was at home [living] with my mom in the hood." Although still in contact with Kanye, Sean would (sometimes) go for months without speaking to his musical mentor. They reportedly sent songs back and forth for review (and even conducted a few business meetings); however, despite over a year of constant contact, Sean had still not been signed to a record label. His pocketbook was beginning to feel the pain.

"I was broke," said Sean. "I would be at McDonald's paying with pennies." He continued, "I would pay for a studio session and not have [enough] money for food." Money was scarce—but not for long. Sean's diligence produced dividends when—after two long years of uncertainty—Kanye West *finally* offered him a recording contract. During the summer of 2007, Big Sean became the newest artist signed to Kanye West's record label G.O.O.D. Music. He would now *officially* join forces with rap royalty. Those two years of struggle proved to be worth it.

Over the next several years, Big Sean would collaborate with Kanye West on hit songs such as "Blessings," "Clique," and "One Man Can Change the World." His musical hero was now a close friend. Reflecting on his journey, Big Sean said the following:

"I used to ride to school listening to Kanye, Jay Z, Lil' Wayne, and Pharrell. Now I can sit back and call them my friends."

Friends with Pharrell. Collaborating with Jay Z. None of this would have happened if Big Sean had not driven down to that Detroit, Michigan, radio station and rapped for Kanye West. In just a few short years, Big Sean went from literally paying with pennies at McDonald's to selling out arenas with the hip hop elite. For these are the results of immediate action.

As you can see from the aforementioned case study, immediate action can dramatically change your life. It is **the fastest way to get from where you** are to where you want to be. But what if you don't want to be a famous rapper? What if you simply want to make a living as an artist or travel the world without having to worry about money? Well—if that is the case—then this next case study is for you! Let's take a look at how entrepreneur Colin Wright travels the world full time without being a multi-millionaire.

Case Study: Colin Wright

"My goal was to make my first million dollars before I was 25—<u>then</u> I would travel the world."
—Colin Wright

Exhausted from his 12-hour workdays as a result of his demanding clientele, entrepreneur Colin Wright was growing steadily frustrated with both his life and his business. He was running a branding studio in Los Angeles, California, frantically servicing a seamlessly endless stream of clients all with one goal in mind: to become a millionaire. "My goal was to make my first million dollars before I was 25—*then* I would travel the world," said Colin during his 2011 TEDx talk. He continued, "I was trying to work my way out of working." It wasn't until several years later, however, that Colin discovered the truth. "I was aiming toward the wrong goal," he said. What Colin *really* wanted was freedom. Freedom to explore himself. Freedom to be an artist. Freedom to travel the world full time—whether he was a millionaire or not.

But how could he attain such freedom? How could Colin travel the world full time without having a million dollars in the bank? Well, the answer was fairly simple. "I sold or got rid of everything I owned that didn't fit into a carry-on bag. I scaled my business so that I could operate it from a laptop instead of from an office," said Colin. He started a blog, or a public website on which he regularly posted personal photography, artwork, and/or writing samples. He slowly gained a following; and, currently, he lives in a different country every four months, in a location voted on by his readers.

Colin had finally gained the freedom he so desperately desired. He was now both a full time artist and a full time world traveler. He had now created a life of freedom, adventure, and self-expression. None of this would have been possible, however, if he had not asked himself the following question: how can I travel the world full time without being a millionaire?

The aforementioned question asked by Colin Wright is what I like to call **the actionable inquiry**. An actionable inquiry is simply a question that leads to immediate action. It is most frequently structured in the following manner: how can I achieve my goal without enduring a particular pain? In other words, the structure is as follows: how can I (insert goal) without (insert avoidable pain or limiting belief)? To better understand this concept, take a look at the following actionable inquiries:

1. How can I make more money **without** working longer hours?
2. How can I start a business **without** sacrificing time with my family?
3. How can I lose weight **without** going to the gym?
4. How can I write a bestselling book **without** being an internationally known celebrity?

In Inquiry #1, a mid-level associate desires to make an extra $1,000 per month within the next three (3) months without having to work longer hours. Perhaps, this associate could get a better paying job, apply for a different position within the same company, ask for a raise, or even quit his current job and demand higher wages as a consultant. The possibilities are endless! Making more money, however, does not (necessarily) have to equate to working longer hours.

In Inquiry #2, an aspiring entrepreneur desires to acquire his first customer within the next four (4) weeks without sacrificing valuable time with his family. Perhaps, this future business owner could build his clientele before his wife wakes up in the morning or after he has put the children to bed at night. He could even start a family business and get the entire household involved! The point is that he does not have to sacrifice time with his family in order to start a business.

In Inquiry #3, a young lady desires to lose 30 pounds within the next six (6) months without going to the gym. Perhaps, this lady could regularly consume 1,900 calories or less, increase her water intake (which raises her metabolism), and consume all carbohydrates (if any) before 2 P.M. Any of these strategies could cause her to burn fat and lose a significant amount of weight without ever having to purchase a gym membership.

In Inquiry #4, an up-and-coming writer aspires to sell 10,000 copies of his first book within one week without having 20 million Twitter followers! Perhaps, this author could organize an affiliate/pre-launch campaign, assemble a passionate launch team, recruit book ambassadors, and/or contact media influencers with audiences interested in the book's subject matter. The historic use of these strategies proves that an author does not have to be famous in order to sell books.

For clarification purposes, **the actionable inquiry was *not* designed to make you any less disciplined or to encourage your participation in short-term success schemes**. It was designed, however, to help you overcome limiting beliefs and to challenge conventional thinking while accelerating your progress toward creating the life you truly want. Use this strategy responsibly.

Create an Action Plan

Now that you fully understand how to form an actionable inquiry, it is essential that you use it to develop your action plan. Your action plan is the foundation of your future and the birthplace of your behavior. It is the cornerstone of creation and the pathway to productivity. Develop your master plan by following these three (3) steps to immediate action.

Step 1: **Develop your actionable inquiry.** Use the aforementioned framework to form an empowering inquiry that leads to immediate action.

Step 2: **Prepare an action list.** Make a list of 5-10 activities that you can complete in order to achieve your goal.

Step 3: **Get to work!** Begin completing the actions on your list.

To demonstrate this simple framework, take a look at what could have been Colin Wright's actionable inquiry and action list:

How can I travel the world full time without being a millionaire?

- ✓ Sell personal items/liquidate assets
- ✓ Close bricks-and-mortar studio
- ✓ Start online business
- ✓ Create more products and/or offer fewer services
- ✓ Use travel rewards credit cards

Colin's action list clearly included selling some of his personal items and transferring his offline business into an online enterprise. His list also included leveraging credit card promotions in order to (legally) gain free airline miles. One other key activity was creating more products while simultaneously offering fewer services. This small yet significant adjustment to his business model allowed him to automate his income and to spend more time travelling, which resulted in the freedom that he so desperately desired.

> **Note:** You may refer to the customizable immediate action agenda found at **www.danmcdaniel.net/action** to develop your own actionable inquiry and to prepare your list of action items.

Too afraid to take action?

Sometimes, the idea of actually taking action on your goals is a very frightening experience. You may become plagued with self-doubt, feelings of inferiority, and even fear of success. Be aware that these feelings are normal and should, in fact, be expected. The truth, however, may be that **your**

inaction is the root cause of your deepest fears. Whenever you get afraid, or (perhaps) become overwhelmed with the idea of taking action, think of the following passage from Norman Vincent Peale:

> _"Action is a great restorer and builder of confidence. Inaction is not only the result, but the cause, of fear. Perhaps the action you take will be successful; perhaps different action or adjustments will have to follow. But any action is better than no action at all."_

Wow! What a statement. Now that you have discovered the possible cause of your fears and prepared a solid action plan, it is time for you to integrate these activities into your daily life. Continue reading to discover how to turn immediate action into long-lasting success.

Step 6:

Develop positive habits.

"Success is the sum of small efforts, repeated day in and day out."
—Robert Collier

The sixth step in the process of achieving your goals is developing positive habits. According to *The American Heritage Dictionary of the English Language*, a habit is defined as "a recurrent, often unconscious, pattern of behavior that is acquired through frequent repetition." This frequent repetition embeds a specific habit into your subconscious and quickly begins to control your entire life. According to Darren Hardy, publisher of *Success Magazine* and author of *The Compound Effect*, your life is the direct result of small, seemingly insignificant choices that add up over time. Your body, your income, and your relationships are generally not determined by a single moment in time but by the "compound effect" of small decisions made one moment at a time. **Your choices become your habits, and your habits become your life.**

Choices ⟶ Habits ⟶ LIFE

This concept was, perhaps, best illustrated by Chinese philosopher Lao Tzu (pronounced loud → zoo) when he said the following: **"Watch your actions; they become habit. Watch your <u>habits</u>; they become character. Watch your character; it becomes your destiny."**

Because your habits become your destiny, it is essential that you develop the habits that will get you closer to the life you want. Continue reading to discover how to make the attainment of your ultimate goal practically inevitable.

Reach Daily Milestones

"Nothing is particularly hard if you divide it into small jobs."
—Henry Ford

Because you learned in chapter one how to make your goals both specific and measurable, you are now capable of breaking down your most important goal into daily performance indicators, or milestones. These milestones allow you to track your progress and make the attainment of your yearly, quarterly, monthly, and weekly goals practically inevitable. The following are examples of common goals and the daily milestones, or habits, necessary to attain them:

Goal: Lose 20 pounds in three (3) months
Habit: Run (or walk) for 30 minutes each day

 Goal: Get my first customer within the next two (2) weeks
Habit: Send out at least three (3) business proposals each day

Goal: Write a book in six (6) months
Habit: Write 500 words per day

The practice of setting (and reaching) daily milestones will slowly yet *consistently* get you closer to achieving your goals and creating the life you truly want. Whether your goal is, to lose weight, to start a business, or to write a book, **developing a positive habit that corresponds with your most important goal is, perhaps, the most effective long-term strategy in the goal-setting arsenal.** Continue reading to discover how Chris Guillebeau (pronounced gill-a-bow) built a publishing empire by simply developing one key habit.

Case Study: Chris Guillebeau

On Wednesday, March 5, 2008, entrepreneur and full time traveler Chris Guillebeau decided to embark on a challenging adventure. In addition to pursuing his goal of travelling to every country in the world, Chris had now adopted a new habit of writing 1,000 words per day. Reaching this daily milestone ensured that he would become a prolific writer and a noted authority in the areas of travel and entrepreneurship. This one habit of writing 1,000 words per day, six days per week, enabled Chris to write approximately 300,000 words each year!

300,000 words x 7 years = 2.1 million words written!

"Writing 300,000 words ensures that I can write a book every year, 100+ blog posts, 50 or so guest posts elsewhere, at least 2-3 business projects that require a lot of writing, and a few long-form essays or magazine pieces," said Chris in 2011. He often surpasses his 1,000-word benchmark but rarely does he produce fewer than his self-imposed minimum word count. When describing how this habit has transformed both his life and his career, Chris said the following:

"Since March 5, 2008, I've tried to follow a practice of writing 1,000 words per day. This practice hasn't always been 100% consistent, but it has helped more than anything else in <u>building a powerful habit</u> and eventually establishing a career."

And what a career it has been. Just two years after developing this habit, Chris Guillebeau published his first book *The Art of Non-Conformity*. Two years after that—in May 2012—he published his second book *The $100 Startup*. This book quickly became an international bestseller and catapulted Chris's career into the stratosphere. By 2014, Chris Guillebeau's books had been read by over 300,000 people, translated into more than 20 different languages, and debuted on both *The New York Times* and *The Wall Street Journal* best seller lists. Approximately 2.1 million words later, he sits atop a publishing empire with both influence and admiration from readers in all 193 countries in which he has visited. All of this became possible simply because he wrote 1,000 words per day. For this is the power of developing positive habits.

———————————

As you can see from the aforementioned case study, developing positive habits can completely transform your life. Positive habits can take you from obesity to fitness, from poverty to affluence, and from obscurity to fame. Personal development pioneer Earl Nightingale often referred to developing positive habits as "the common denominator of success." In his groundbreaking audio program *Lead the Field*, he described positive habit formation as "the determining factor in any outstanding achievement of any kind." These statements made by the titan of personal transformation prove that long-lasting success results from your application of (and your answer to) the following question: **what is the <u>one habit</u> that I can develop that will get me closer to my most important goal?**

For this is the ultimate question. It is now your job to determine the one activity that—if completed each day—will get you closer to the life you ultimately want. **Refer to the fill-in-the-blank daily habit tracker found at <u>www.danmcdaniel.net/action</u> to brainstorm possible answers to this question**, and continue reading to discover how developing positive habits can lead to life-changing opportunities as a result of seemingly unstoppable momentum.

Step 7:

Gain momentum.

"My definition of luck is preparation meeting the moment of opportunity."

—Oprah Winfrey

The seventh step in the process of achieving your goals is gaining momentum. Momentum is defined as "the force or speed at which a series of events takes place." It is the rapid movement toward a specific goal. Often characterized by life-changing opportunities, or so-called "lucky" breaks, momentum typically manifests itself in the form of new relationships and career-defining moments. It is gained as the result of a lifetime of immediate action and positive habit formation.

A somewhat elusive phenomenon, the momentum principle is often unforeseen in the eyes of its beholder. It shows up when you are deep "in the trenches," diligently working toward your most important goal. When you are experiencing momentum, you may feel like your life is going in "fast motion," as if you are riding on a roller coaster at The Amusement Park of Opportunity. To better illustrate this principle, let's take a look at how momentum created life-altering opportunities for entertainment icon Jennifer Lopez.

Case Study: Jennifer Lopez

"It was fast and furious after that [first album]. My life went into fast motion."

—Jennifer Lopez

While working at a law firm and studying business at Baruch College in Manhattan, soon-to-be entertainment icon Jennifer Lopez had a dream. According to her 2010 interview with VH1's *Behind the Music*, Jennifer recalls having a dream, waking up, and then telling her parents the following: "I had a dream that I'm supposed to be in the entertainment industry. I'm supposed to be in show business, and I don't want to go to college next month." Frustrated and confused, Jennifer's mother Guadalupe did not respond in favor. "We got in a huge fight," said Guadalupe. This confrontation was so huge, in fact, that it resulted in Jennifer's moving out of her childhood home and onto the unforgiving streets of New York City.

Determined to make it at all costs, Jennifer immersed herself into performance art. "I was literally obsessed with dancing. I took classes day and night," said Jennifer. She was so obsessed, in fact, that she actually moved into the dance studio for a brief period of time. **Surviving off one-dollar pizzas and sleeping on a bench in a dance studio were the small beginnings of a larger-than-life career for Jennifer Lopez.** Over the next few years, she paid her dues by dancing on television series, in music videos, and on stage with some of the biggest names in music.

Some vintage footage of Lopez shows her performing at the 1991 American Music Awards with New Kids on the Block, dancing on the 90s hit series *In Living Color*, and even performing in Janet Jackson's iconic 1993 music video "That's the Way Love Goes." In 1994, after attending a multitude of auditions, Lopez finally landed her first acting job as a store clerk in the short-lived television series *South Central.* Although the show was cancelled after only one season, Lopez herself became inundated with opportunity. "I decided not to go back [on tour with Janet Jackson] because I got my first acting job, and then **things just went like a roller coaster** from there," said Lopez.

That "roller coaster" that she mentioned took her from minor acting jobs to supporting roles in feature films such as *Money Train* and *Blood and Wine.*

This momentum even led to her breakout role in the 1997 musical biopic *Selena*. It was this role that would catapult her into superstardom. "When *Selena* hit, [my career] went into overdrive." Lopez continued, "My life had changed completely." As a now-bonafide superstar and critically acclaimed actress, Lopez began landing leading roles in major motion pictures, a trend that would continue for the next two decades of her career. As a testament to her tremendous growth as an actress, let's take a look at her movie earnings during the first decade of her acting career.

Movie Earnings for Jennifer Lopez

Year	Movie	Salary
2005	Monster-in-Law	$ 15,000,000
2002	Maid in Manhattan	$ 12,000,000
2002	Enough	$ 10,000,000
2001	The Wedding Planner	$ 9,000,000
2000	The Cell	$ 4,000,000
1998	Out of Sight	$ 2,000,000
1997	Selena	$ 1,000,000
1996	Blood and Wine	$ 250,000
1995	Money Train	$ 200,000
1995	My Family	$ 50,000

source: IMDb

Now, suddenly **overwhelmed with opportunity,** Jennifer Lopez was experiencing <u>the momentum principle</u>. After spending 10 years in near-obscurity, she was now finally capitalizing on these possibly fleeting moments of good fortune. Jennifer's manager, Benny Medina, described his experience with momentum as follows:

"It seemed like [Jennifer and I] were <u>always</u> in a recording studio, <u>always</u> on a movie set, <u>always</u> at a photoshoot, <u>always</u> on a plane... we were so busy <u>doing</u> that we were not even thinking about the impossible [achievements] that were actually being accomplished."

One of those "impossible achievements" occurred in January 2001 when Jennifer Lopez became the first entertainer in history to have both a number one album, *J.Lo*, and a number one movie, *The Wedding Planner*, released during the same week. According to her NUVOtv documentary *Jennifer Lopez: Her Life. Her Journey.*, she has sold over 75 million albums, and her movies have grossed over $2 billion worldwide. In just 14 years, **Jennifer Lopez went from sleeping on a bench in a dance studio to setting world records among the Hollywood elite.** From struggling dancer to film-making icon, life-changing opportunities and career-defining relationships have created the phenomenon known as Jennifer Lopez. For these are the results of momentum.

Momentum is an elusive phenomenon. It cannot be practiced—it can only be *experienced*. It is co-created between you and the Universe only after you have spent significant time *consistently* working toward your most important goal. Once momentum is in your grasp, even the most ambitious of your constituents cannot duplicate your results. For it is of divine nature, of the purest intent, and only bestowed upon those who rightly deserve it. Continue to step eight to discover how to earn the results of momentum.

Step 8:

Be patient.

"Any solid achievement must of necessity take years of humble apprenticeship and estrangement from most of society."
—Gerald Sykes

In order for momentum to properly take effect, you must be willing to be patient. Practicing patience will ensure that you meet success with a humble heart and a wise spirit. Exhibiting the essential virtue of patience allows you to master your craft and manifest your destiny. With evidence in the form of classic books such as *Mastery* by Robert Greene and *Outliers* by Malcolm Gladwell, it has been proven that long-term success is the result of long-term apprenticeship.

Becoming a great leader in your field requires that you first become a great student. Few people embody this concept better than media mogul Oprah Winfrey. Take a look at how she combined the patience principle with the art of apprenticeship to go from a part-time job at a local radio station to the owner of a billion-dollar media empire that inspires millions of people worldwide.

Case Study: Oprah Winfrey

"That was my after-school job—working at the radio station at 16 years old."

—Oprah Winfrey

Born in 1954—the same year that segregated schools were ruled unconstitutional in the United States of America—soon-to-be media mogul Oprah Winfrey began her quest for world domination. By 1957, she was already a public speaking sensation in her local community. "When I was three years old, I was speaking in the church," said Oprah in 2001. She continued, "My broadcasting career [really] started in the church." Not held back by the racial limitations of the pre-Civil Rights Movement, Oprah was able to excel in school and develop her natural talents. "My sense of validation came early on in life from being smart, from being able to read, and from being able to speak [well] in public," she said. Although she did not know during childhood, these abilities would later launch her into superstardom.

By age 16, Oprah was busy managing her time between academics and charity. Eager to find a business to sponsor her in a March of Dimes walkathon, she walked into the Nashville, Tennessee, radio station WVOL to ask for sponsorship. While in the process of inquiring, one of the station's employees, John Heidelberg, became completely enamored of her. He was captivated by her intelligence and her speaking abilities. Incredibly impressed, he thought that she would make an excellent newsperson. Oprah then agreed to John's recommendation of reading some news copy on tape. The entire station of broadcasters was so impressed by Oprah's speaking voice that she was hired immediately. "I was hired *that* day," Oprah said. "That was my after-school job—working at the radio station at 16 years old."

By 1971, Oprah's broadcasting career had become both a viable source of income and a viable source of opportunity. "I was making $10,000 per year in 1971," said Oprah in a 2014 interview at the Stanford Graduate School of Business. She leveraged her experience at the radio station to land her first job as a television news anchor at age 19. "The first semester of my sophomore year [in college], I started working in news," said Oprah.

While still enrolled as a college student in Nashville, Oprah *prematurely* got the opportunity of a lifetime. "I got an offer to go to Atlanta for $40,000 [per year]," she said. The soon-to-be birthplace of 24-hour news network CNN, Atlanta, Georgia, was a broadcasting boon. Although grateful for the opportunity, she declined. Both Oprah and her then-boss believed that she needed to remain in Nashville to "perfect her craft" as a journalist. As a result of this decision, she became a much better writer, an even-better speaker, and an overall highly-skilled news anchor prepared for even the biggest of opportunities. For her patience had fostered preparation.

By 1976, however, Oprah was ready for a change. "I felt that I had grown enough in Nashville and couldn't grow anymore, so I moved to Baltimore," she said. At age 22—making $22,000 per year—Oprah seemed to be flourishing in her chosen profession. That was not the case, however, in 1978. "I got a huge demotion," said Oprah. She continued, "I was doing the 6 o' clock news, and they placed me on the new local talk show that was starting called *People Are Talking*." After the very first taping of the show, Oprah's "huge demotion" turned into a huge breakthrough in terms of self-discovery.

"I came off that stage on August 14, 1978, and I knew that I was home." Oprah explained, "It felt like home because it felt so natural." She added, "It was the most natural I had ever felt at work." Oprah would remain in Baltimore for five more years, further developing her expertise and her natural talents as an on-air personality. Now, with 13 solid years of experience in broadcasting, it was time for another challenge. Now an industry veteran, she was thoroughly prepared for the next level of achievement.

Meanwhile, in Chicago, television station turnaround king Dennis Swanson was faced with a dilemma. He was the newly-appointed vice president of WLS-TV, and the station was failing miserably. "The station was a mess," said Swanson in a 2012 interview at Boston University. "We were last [in the ratings], and they sent me there to fix it." Swanson's number one priority was to find new talent. Receiving notice of the open position from a former producer, Oprah auditioned for the job during Labor Day Weekend 1983. Four months later, she began as the new host of *A.M. Chicago*. Reflecting on the results of this change in talent, Swanson said the following: "We went from last to first [in the ratings] in one month, which is almost un-heard-of."

By September 1985, *A.M. Chicago* was renamed *The Oprah Winfrey Show*. Just one year later—on September 8, 1986—*The Oprah Winfrey Show* began its national syndication. "We were successful *immediately*," said Oprah in 2005. "We were so successful so quickly [that] it was stunning—even to *me*." This "immediate success," however, only came after years of patience and apprenticeship. Take a look at this brief timeline of Oprah's broadcasting career:

1954 – Born in Mississippi during the first year of the Civil Rights Movement

1957 – Began speaking in church at age 3

1970 – **Began first job at radio station at age 16**

1973 – Began television career as a news anchor at age 19

1976 – Moved to Baltimore, Maryland, at age 22

1978 – Began as co-host of *People Are Talking* at age 24

1983 – Auditioned for Dennis Swanson at age 29

1984 – Began hosting *A.M. Chicago* at age 30

1985 – Renamed *A.M. Chicago* to *The Oprah Winfrey Show* at age 31

1986 – **Began national syndication of *The Oprah Winfrey Show* at age 32**

2011 – Ends *The Oprah Winfrey Show* and launches OWN: The Oprah Winfrey Network at age 57

As you can see from the timeline above, Oprah began working in the broadcasting industry at age 16. *The Oprah Winfrey Show* didn't begin its national syndication until Oprah was 32 years old. This means that **it took Oprah 16 years to attain "immediate success."** Before she got her first million-dollar check, she had been working in the broadcasting industry for *literally* half her life! Beginning in 1970 and continuing into 2011 and beyond, **it has taken more than 40 years (over four decades!) for her to reach this level of achievement**. One step at a time, Oprah has built a billion-dollar empire that inspires people from all around the world. For these are the results of practicing patience.

As you can see from the aforementioned case study, it often takes a lifetime of work to prepare for one moment of divine opportunity. Through patience and apprenticeship, you can ensure that you are adequately prepared for your supreme moment of destiny. If you only remember one statement from this chapter, remember this: success comes quickly but only after you have developed *slowly*. I repeat: **success comes quickly but only after you have developed *slowly*.** For total transformation occurs in an instant. Continue reading to discover the two remaining elements of success.

Step 9:

Become an epic failure.

"Only those who dare to fail greatly can ever achieve greatly."
—Robert F. Kennedy

The ninth step in the process of achieving your goals is becoming an epic failure. Failure is defined as "the state or condition of not meeting a desirable or intended objective." It is the attainment of disappointing results. While on your journey toward the life you want, you will <u>inevitably</u> be disappointed. You will <u>inevitably</u> **fall flat on your face**. You will <u>inevitably</u> *fail*. It is the lessons of failure, however, that prepare you for the <u>celebration</u> of success.

It is through trial and error that you design the life you want. The problem, however, may be that you were previously unaware of this step in the process. Contrary to popular belief, failure is not to be avoided—it is to be *expected*. In most cases, you must undergo short-term failure in order to experience long-term success. Few people embody this principle better than world-renowned financial advisor Suze Orman. Let's take a look at how she navigated failure while on her journey from rejected writer to *New York Times* bestselling author.

Case Study: Suze Orman

"Three weeks into [the book tour], no one showed up to __any__ of my book signings—not one person."
—Suze Orman

Before becoming a one-woman book publishing powerhouse, Suze Orman was just a California-based financial advisor. Approached by book agent Linda Mead at a 1994 cocktail party, Suze agreed to share her expertise in a book. As an expert on long term care insurance, Suze wanted to write a book that captured the essence of her clientele—people aged 65 and over. The working title of her book, therefore, became *Keeping Your Gold in the Golden Years*, with the "golden years" referring to life after retirement.

Excited to have a new client, Suze's agent and future co-author Linda Mead began pitching their book to publishers. Unfortunately, however, New York City publishing executives were not interested. According to Suze, they did not want to publish a financial book written by a woman. Because of this, **Suze's first book was turned down by over 30 publishers**. "We were turned down by every single major publisher out there—except for one," said Suze in a 2012 interview. In addition to a $10,000 book advance, pint-sized publishing company Newmarket Press published Suze's first book later re-titled *You've Earned It, Don't Lose It* in January 1995. After a solid year of writing and development, the book was finally available to the public.

In an effort to promote *You've Earned It, Don't Lose It*, Suze's publisher advised her to go on a 27-city book tour. Although much to Suze's dismay, she agreed. The public, however, could not have cared less. "Three weeks into [the book tour], no one showed up to *any* of my book signings—not one person," said Suze. Because no one ever showed up, Suze gave her speech to the book sellers. These librarians, distributors, and event organizers were so moved by Suze's financial intelligence that they began to recommend her book to readers. "The first print run was 15,000 [copies]," said Suze. "Within just a few weeks, all 15,000 books were sold."

With multiple copies of *You've Earned It, Don't Lose It* now in circulation, Suze's publisher convinced Q2, a subsidiary of QVC, to promote the book. "QVC didn't like books because [an author] couldn't demonstrate a book," said Suze. She continued, "They had every major author on QVC, and they all flopped terribly." The payment history of the network indicates that only cookbooks would perform well because the author's recipes *could* be properly demonstrated on a television platform. With knowledge of a high chance of failure, Suze decided to appear on the network anyway. She reportedly told true stories about her clients—case studies, if you will—and their various battles with estate planning. These real-life stories about wills, trusts, taxes, and long term care insurance connected with the hearts of viewers, and books actually sold.

After 20 minutes on the air, Suze had sold exactly 303 books on Q2. Although this may sound like a small figure, this was a tremendous feat for the new author. For she had broken the proverbial "curse" of both new and established authors on Q2. Astonished by Suze's success, Q2 book buyer Paula Piercy contacted QVC's director of merchandising, Karen Fonner, and the two conspired to get Suze in front of a larger audience. Shortly after their conversation, Suze appeared on QVC. The following are the results of her first three appearances on the program:

1st appearance → sold **2,500** books in **8** minutes
2nd appearance → sold **4,400** books in **10** minutes
3rd appearance → sold **10,000** books in **12** minutes

You've Earned It, Don't Lose It went on to sell more than 160,000 copies on QVC alone. The runaway success of Suze's first book led to a six-figure bidding war for her second book *The 9 Steps to Financial Freedom*. "The 9 Steps to Financial Freedom sold [to Crown Publishing Group] for $800,000," said Suze in 2011. In March 1997, the first time QVC had ever dedicated an entire hour's show to one book, viewers purchased 25,000 copies of *The 9 Steps to Financial Freedom*. "In one hour, we sold $680,000 worth of books," said Suze. That book went on to sell over 300,000 copies in 1997 and over 3 million copies worldwide over the next decade. According to Publishers Weekly, *The 9 Steps to Financial Freedom* was the number one bestselling nonfiction book of 1998.

"The book was a phenomenon," said Suze. This "phenomenon" ignited her public profile and took her from hour-long segments on QVC to record-breaking fundraisers on PBS to life-changing breakthroughs on *The Oprah Winfrey Show*. Suze became such a fixture in the world of personal finance that she began her own self-titled series, *The Suze Orman Show*, on CNBC in 2002.

In 1994, **Suze's first book was rejected by over 30 publishers**. In 1995, no one showed up to her first book signing. By 1998, she had the number one bestselling nonfiction book in the United States of America. By 2012, she had sold over 30 million books as the author of nine consecutive *New York Times* bestsellers. **This means that, <u>for every publisher who rejected her in 1994</u>, she has sold over one million copies of her books.** "You do not have 30 million copies of books in circulation if they haven't changed lives," said Suze in 2012. In just four years, Suze went from rejected writer to world-renowned author and catalyst of personal transformation. <u>It was because of a failed book tour that Suze discovered the platform that would spread her message to millions of readers worldwide.</u> For this is how epic failure can turn into massive success.

As you can see from the aforementioned case study, massive success is, sometimes, the result of epic failure. It is failure that consistently humbles your ego and softens your soul. These gut-wrenching disappointments and character-building setbacks ensure that you meet success with a keen heart and a deserving spirit. For the lessons of failure prepare you for the celebration of success. Continue reading to discover the final step in the process of achieving your goals.

Step 10:

Practice persistence.

"It's always too early to quit."
—Norman Vincent Peale

The final step in the process of achieving your goals is practicing persistence. According to the *Oxford American College Dictionary*, persistence is defined as "firm continuance in a chosen course of action in spite of difficulty or opposition." It is the act of relentlessly pursuing your goal over a long period of time. While practicing persistence, there will be several occasions during which you consider giving up. You will *undoubtedly* be challenged, tried, tested, and deterred. It is your willingness to regain your direction, however, that will ultimately give you the victory.

While on the journey toward the life you want, you will experience moments of temporary defeat. You may experience a **health** crisis, a **financial** crisis, a **relationship** crisis, or even a **career** crisis. Regardless of its area of impact, experiencing a major life crisis while on the path toward achieving your goals is almost *inevitable*. Although largely unavoidable and almost certain to happen, these major life events develop within you an unrivaled tenacity and a penetrating persistence. It is these characteristics that will help you persevere during the storm.

Persevere During the Storm

"When everything seems to be going against you, remember that the airplane takes off against the wind, not with it."
—Henry Ford

As proven through countless stories of achievement, life often gets the hardest right before a breakthrough. This period of hardship is known as "the storm." During the great storm of your life, you must find the strength to persevere. For The Rainbow of Good Fortune only appears after the clouds have departed. You must prove to the Universe that you are worthy of the rainbow by persevering through the storm. Let's take a look at how music icon Kanye West deemed himself worthy of elite status within the recording industry by persevering through a life-threatening medical emergency.

Case Study: Kanye West

"Even from his hospital bed, Kanye was thinking of raps… thinking of ways to be successful."
—Warren Trotter
Grammy Award-winning songwriter, rapper, and close friend of Kanye West

With his name meaning "the only one," connoisseur of controversy Kanye West grew up in the suburbs of South Side, Chicago. While enrolled at Chicago State University, he reportedly spent most of his time in the recording studio. This investment of time led to Kanye's producing his first major beat on Jermaine Dupri's 1998 debut studio album *Life in 1472*. Only 20 years old (and still living with his mother), he reportedly received $5,000 for his efforts. This early success convinced Kanye that he was destined for superstardom. His work with Jermaine Dupri led to a meeting with recording industry giant Columbia Records, and Kanye risked everything for this potentially life-changing opportunity.

"He believed so much that he was going to get a record deal that he dropped out of school with no [backup] plan," said producer Dion Wilson.

Overflowing with confidence, Kanye got flown out to New York City to meet with Columbia Records executives. Unfortunately, however, his arrogance got the best of him. He reportedly spoke negatively about other artists on the record label, in hopes of convincing Columbia executives that both he and his music were superior. Unsurprisingly, this strategy did not work. Kanye walked out of the meeting without a recording contract and never heard from Columbia again. "Kanye pulled up in a limousine and rode away in a taxi," said rapper Cheland Smith half-jokingly. Disappointed by the meeting's outcome, he returned home to Chicago and got very serious about his craft.

"Kanye didn't go to parties. All he did was sit in his room and make beats," said his friend Jasper. He reportedly increased his production fees and worked as a ghost producer, developing beats that were published under other producers' names. Frustrated by his lack of success in Chicago, Kanye moved to Newark, New Jersey. Renting an apartment just 20 minutes away from New York City, he focused intensely on music production. Kanye began producing beats for so many artists signed with Roc-A-Fella Records that he was given unrestricted access to the label's recording studio. Just a few months after moving near New York City, Kanye had penetrated the recording industry's inner circle. For his hustle was paying off.

While delivering music one day at the recording studio, Kanye ran into Roc-A-Fella Records co-founder and soon-to-be rap legend Jay Z. Jay Z enjoyed the music that Kanye delivered, and the two began recording together. By the end of their multiple recording sessions, **Kanye had produced 5 out of 15 songs on Jay Z's album**. This Jay Z album on which Kanye produced one-third of the tracks was called *The Blueprint*. Critically acclaimed and hailed as **one of the greatest hip-hop albums of all time**, *The Blueprint* put Kanye West on the map as a music producer. "Every major artist in urban music was requesting music from Kanye," said Kanye's assistant Devo Harris. Although in demand as a producer, Kanye was not respected as a rapper. Leveraging the success of *The Blueprint*, Kanye reportedly went into every record label—*literally* from A to Z—in search of a recording contract. He was denied by every single label from **A**rista to **Z**omba because industry executives felt that he was incapable of successfully transitioning from music producer to music artist. Kanye was beginning to lose hope.

Solely because he did not want to lose Kanye as a producer, Roc-A-Fella Records co-founder Damon Dash *finally* signed Kanye as a music artist in August 2002. Just two months later, however, Kanye's life took a near-fatal turn. On Wednesday, October 23, 2002—at approximately 3:00 A.M., according to MTV News—**Kanye West was involved in a life-threatening car accident**. On the way to his hotel after a late-night recording session, Kanye lost control of the wheel and collided head-on with another vehicle. Kanye's steering wheel reportedly hit him in the face and fractured his jaw in three places. Barely conscious, he got rushed to the emergency room. Doctors presumed that he would have died if the steering wheel had hit him in the nose.

After multiple surgeries, Kanye's face became incredibly swollen. Now, virtually unrecognizable, he could barely even speak. Kanye's mother Donda said the following about his post-surgery appearance:

"When I walked into that hospital room, I wouldn't have even known my own son had he not [mumbled], 'Hi, Mom!' His face was so swollen."

Admitted into Cedars-Sinai Medical Center—the same hospital in which legendary rappers Eazy-E and The Notorious B.I.G. died—he was lucky to be alive. In order for Kanye to eventually make a full recovery, doctors had to re-wire his jaw. This means that Kanye West, a person who makes his living from his voice, could barely even speak. **His doctors had to wire his mouth shut**. Although family and friends were concerned that his budding rap career had ended (before it really even began), Kanye remained undeterred.

Kanye reportedly waited only one day after his surgery to get back to work. "Even from his hospital bed, Kanye was thinking of raps... thinking of ways to be successful," said his co-writer and friend Warren Trotter. Immediately after leaving the hospital, Kanye checked himself into The W Hotel and built a makeshift studio in his hotel room. Just two weeks after his near-fatal car accident, Kanye recorded his debut single "Through the Wire."

Perfectly describing Kanye's perseverance during this time period, former Capitol Records talent scout Joe Weinberger said the following: "**He literally rapped <u>through the wire</u> while his mouth was still wired shut**."

Kanye's recording industry peers were astonished by his public display of tenacity. "It sounded like it hurt when he rapped," said fellow rapper Ludacris. "He couldn't even open his mouth fully—it was crazy!" said Kanye's co-writer Malik Yusef. Undeterred by a life-threatening car accident, Kanye had proven that he was "wired" for success. Although, now respected by his peers, record label executives remarkably *still* did not believe in his ability as a rapper. Because of this, Kanye decided to become the master of his fate.

To prove that he was worthy of a mainstream album release date, Kanye produced and recorded his 2003 mixtape *Get Well Soon....* This independently released album included the single "Through the Wire." Using the money he earned as a music producer, Kanye spent $40,000 to shoot a music video for this song. Premiering at The 40/40 Club in New York City, he invited numerous recording industry executives and members of the press. Roc-A-Fella executives were impressed by his promotional efforts and finally agreed to release his album. Described by Jay Z as "groundbreaking," Kanye's debut album, *The College Dropout*, was released on February 10, 2004.

According to the Recording Industry Association of America (RIAA), *The College Dropout* was certified platinum on April 6, 2004, selling one million copies worldwide. Just two months later—on June 30, 2004—it was certified double platinum, selling more than two million copies worldwide. *The College Dropout* even earned Kanye the 2005 Grammy Award for Best Rap Album. Former Capitol Records talent scout Joe Weinberger said the following about Kanye's post-debut album phenomenon: "**It was Kanye West pandemonium. He instantly became the number one-talked-about thing in music**."

In just six years, Kanye West went from rejected rapper to worldwide phenomenon. He utilized the principle of perseverance to rise above personal challenges and achieve his lifelong dreams. On Saturday, June 15, 2013—more than a decade after undergoing reconstructive surgery *at the same hospital*—Kanye's then-girlfriend and television personality Kim Kardashian gave birth to their daughter North West at Cedars-Sinai Medical Center in Los

Angeles, California. In less than 11 years, Kanye West went from a life-threatening car accident to a life-creating partnership. For these are the results of persevering through the storm.

Persevering through the storm has a wide range of benefits. It allows you to develop character, to harness tenacity, and to reap the rewards of your lifelong labor. Practicing persistence proves that you are worthy of opportunity and deserving of good fortune. While practicing persistence, however, you must also be willing to change your approach.

Change Your Approach

Sometimes, persistence just isn't enough. Occasionally, you may need to change your approach. Consider this option during the moments when perseverance continuously renders you the same results. Often, a small tweak in your strategy can create for you a more desirable outcome. These, sometimes, micro-pivots can dramatically impact the direction of your life. Let's take a look at how a small change in media maven Tyler Perry's approach took him from empty theaters to sold-out arenas.

Case Study: Tyler Perry

"Every time we did a show, it failed. And it kept going that way for [nearly] seven years."
—Tyler Perry

Young and ambitious, 22-year-old Tyler Perry moved from New Orleans to Atlanta in 1992 to become a famous playwright. With the ultimate goal of staging a successful play, Tyler invested his life savings into the project. When only 30 people showed up to a 1,200-seat theater, Tyler's $12,000 investment resulted in a negative return. "It was pretty devastating," said Tyler in a 2010 interview with Oprah Winfrey. Frustrated, homeless, and suicidal, Tyler somehow found the strength to carry on.

Living in his car when he could not afford a pay-by-the-week hotel, Tyler worked a series of odd jobs to finance his annual play. "I [have been] a used car salesman, a shoe-shiner, a bartender, and a waiter," said Tyler. Although he had multiple jobs, he would always lose them because he would take time off to produce plays! Unfortunately, these plays resulted in repeated failure. "Every time we did a show, it failed. And it kept going that way for [nearly] seven years," said Perry.

Disheartened and on the verge of giving up, Perry decided to give his play just one last try. This time, though, he would take a different approach. **Instead of relying on promoters to fill theater seats, Perry himself went into the local community to personally recruit attendees.** He visited local churches and persuaded the pastors and members of the choir to participate in his play. This small-yet-crucial shift from traditional advertising to word-of-mouth marketing was the change in approach that would forever define Perry's career.

On March 12, 1998—after six years and six failed attempts at staging the almost-exact same play—Perry had finally achieved success. When he looked outside of the Atlanta House of Blues windows, he saw a long line of eager attendees. According to Perry, viewers were lined up "around the block," an image that he would soon become accustomed to. **Because he had now clearly identified his target market, Perry had developed a system that could be duplicated time and time again.** And that's what he did.

Tyler's play *I Know I've Been Changed* sold out eight times in a row! The venue reportedly became so crowded that he had to move his production to the much larger (and much more prestigious) Fox Theatre located in Midtown Atlanta. Luckily for Perry, this was only the beginning. It was reported by Tyler's official website that 35,000 people per week attended one of his shows in 2005. This means that Tyler Perry went from a theater of 30 people to an audience of 35,000 people *per week* in just 13 years. What a transformation!

Currently, in 2016, you can find Tyler Perry starring in feature films, writing bestselling books, and negotiating syndication deals for his various television series. In 2008, Tyler Perry and his team of developers transformed 30 acres of property into 200,000 square feet of broadcasting bliss in the form of Tyler Perry Studios. With financial security and a pipeline of powerful peers,

Tyler Perry will never have to worry about being homeless again. For this is the power of changing your approach.

_____

As you can see from the aforementioned case study, changing your approach can forever shape your destiny. Small changes to even the most trivial of details have the potential to shift the direction of your life for years to come. When faced with an enduring challenge, don't just persevere—alter your approach. This critical step can help you overcome obstacles and remove barriers time and time again. Continue on to the conclusion for an action-packed summary of the ten steps to meteoric success.

Conclusion:

The Final Step

Now that you know the ten (10) steps to success, you must now complete the final step: **get started**. The process of achieving your goals can never truly begin until *you* begin. Get started on your journey today! To make this process even easier for you, I have developed an all-inclusive action guide that covers each step on your journey. Including a personalized perfect day planner, a fill-in-the-blank daily habit tracker, a customizable immediate action agenda, and a state-of-the-art limiting beliefs eliminator, this 20-page workbook can be instantly downloaded to your smartphone, your tablet, or your computer and printed out for immediate use by visiting **www.danmcdaniel.net/action**.

Completing this final step in the process of achieving your goals requires that you first revisit the original ten (10) steps. From creating a vision to building relationships to developing habits, you have (hopefully) learned a lot from this book. Because of this potentially life-changing overload, I have prepared for you a brief summary of the biggest takeaways from each chapter. Let us now review *The Ultimate Guide to Success: How to Achieve Your Goals in 10 Steps or Less*:

The Final Step

<u>Step 1: Decide what you want</u>. When you have a clear vision of the life you desire as well as a deep understanding of your core values, you are then equipped to begin the journey toward true success and fulfillment. Avoid scattering your resources by selecting the <u>one</u> goal that, if achieved, will have the greatest positive impact on your life. Pursue this <u>one</u> goal and focus on the *feeling* it will give you at the time of its achievement.

<u>Step 2: Have a strong purpose</u>. The three (3) layers of purpose are passion, frustration, and necessity. These fundamental drives of human nature dramatically decrease procrastination and increase motivation. Igniting at least one of these drives is the key to eliminating excuses and defeating the three (3) enemies of achievement.

<u>Step 3: Build solid relationships</u>. The quality of your relationships directly determines your income, your health, and your overall level of happiness. You may improve your relationships by changing your environment, getting a mentor, joining a mastermind group, or getting an accountability partner. It is these relationships that will influence your mindset and determine your future.

<u>Step 4: Establish empowering beliefs</u>. Before you can begin living the life of your dreams, you must first identify the thoughts, the stories, and the behaviors that are holding you back. These false ideas about who you are and what you are capable of have been woven deep into your subconscious as a result of several years of conditioning. Certain <u>events</u>, certain <u>individuals</u>, and even certain <u>environments</u> from your past have all contributed to your current beliefs. It is your job to identify these hidden beliefs so that you can change your story and release the shackles of your past experiences.

<u>Step 5: Take immediate action</u>. Action builds confidence. Inaction causes fear. When you take *immediate* action, you temporarily eradicate all feelings of inferiority and move (with seemingly superhuman capabilities) toward your ultimate destination. Taking immediate action is the fastest route toward getting from where you are to where you want to be.

Step 6: Develop positive habits. Your life is the direct result of small, seemingly insignificant choices that add up over time. These choices *eventually* become your habits, and your habits *eventually* become your life. It is good practice to break down your most important goal into daily habits, or milestones. These milestones allow you to track your progress and make the attainment of your yearly, quarterly, monthly, and weekly goals practically inevitable. Developing a positive habit that corresponds with your most important goal is, perhaps, the most effective long-term strategy in the goal-setting arsenal.

Step 7: Gain momentum. Momentum is the process of rapidly moving toward your goals. Often characterized by life-changing opportunities, or so-called "lucky" breaks, momentum is gained as the result of a lifetime of immediate action and positive habit formation. A somewhat elusive phenomenon, momentum cannot be practiced—it can only be *experienced*. For it is of divine nature, of the purest intent, and only bestowed upon those who rightly deserve it.

Step 8: Be patient. In order for the momentum principle to properly take effect, you must be patient. Long-term success is the result of long-term apprenticeship. For success comes <u>quickly</u> but only after you have developed *slowly*.

Step 9: Become an epic failure. Contrary to popular belief, failure is not to be avoided—it is to be *expected*. In most cases, you must undergo short-term failure in order to experience long-term success. While on your journey toward the life you want, you will <u>inevitably</u> be disappointed. You will <u>inevitably</u> **fall flat on your face**. You will <u>inevitably</u> *fail*. It is the lessons of failure, however, that prepare you for the celebration of success.

The Final Step

<u>Step 10: Practice persistence</u>. While on the journey toward achieving your goals, there will be several occasions during which you consider giving up. You will be *undoubtedly* challenged, tried, tested, and deterred. It is your willingness to regain your direction, however, that will ultimately give you the victory.

Decide what you want. Have a strong purpose. Build solid relationships. Establish empowering beliefs. Take immediate action. Develop positive habits. Gain momentum. Be patient. Become an epic failure. And practice persistence. These are the ten (10) steps to success and the keys to transforming your life. Get started today and begin living the life of your dreams!

Join the Movement!

My goal is to help one million people achieve their goals by 2020. Join me on this mission by doing the following:

<u>Write a book review</u>. Let me (and the entire world) know how this book has changed your life and/or business by posting a review on Amazon.com. Simply visit the book's homepage at <u>www.danmcdaniel.net/book</u>, scroll down to the bottom of the page, click on "Write a customer review," and post your results, your biggest takeaways, and/or your life-changing breakthroughs.

I thank you in advance for spreading positivity. If you have an outstanding story, you might even get the opportunity to be featured in my next book!

<u>Share this book with someone you care about</u>. Pass on these principles to at least one person in your circle of influence—a friend, a colleague, a relative, or even a stranger! Use the gift page at the front of this book to share the principles of success with someone who will appreciate it. (**<u>Note</u>**: *The Ultimate Guide to Success* **makes for an awesome holiday or birthday gift!**)

Special Offer

Save up to 50% off the regular price when you purchase 10 or more paperback books!

The Ultimate Guide to Success: How to Achieve Your Goals in 10 Steps or Less is the most comprehensive book ever written on the subject of success. Drawing on over 5,000 hours of research, this book can help anyone go from where they are to where they want to be.

The following is a list of the types of people who would most benefit from the information in this book:

- High school or college graduates
- Corporate sales executives
- Small business owners
- Aspiring musicians, dancers, actors, athletes, authors, and entrepreneurs
- People experiencing personal difficulties, i.e., homelessness, job loss, injury, illness, etc.
- Anyone who desires a better life for themselves and others

Increase your company's revenue, offer guidance to a promising student, or inspire a group of extraordinary people by visiting the website below.

www.danmcdaniel.net/order

Own <u>The Ultimate Success Series</u>

Get all three (3) books written by Dan McDaniel

Extreme Honesty
Reflections of a Nineteen-Year-Old Philosopher

The Ultimate Guide to Success
How to Achieve Your Goals in 10 Steps or Less

The Life You Want Workbook
A Companion to Dan McDaniel's *The Ultimate Guide to Success*

The Life You Want Workbook
A Companion to Dan McDaniel's *The Ultimate Guide to Success*

Identify Your #1 Goal in 90 Minutes or Less!

The Life You Want Workbook is the must-have companion to Dan McDaniel's blockbuster bestseller *The Ultimate Guide to Success*. Drawing on over 5,000 hours of research, this workbook personalizes the process of achieving your goals. Both **customizable** and **interactive**, *The Life You Want Workbook* is the most valuable resource for planning how you will get from where you are to where you want to be.

Contained within its pages are a personalized perfect day planner, a fill-in-the-blank daily habit tracker, a customizable immediate action agenda, and a state-of-the-art limiting beliefs eliminator. These tools—along with many others—are designed to help you:

- ✓ **Discover what *really* matters to you** (hint: it's probably <u>not</u> what you think),
- ✓ **Identify your #1 biggest obstacle** to achievement (and how to overcome it),
- ✓ Recognize your **unique value** to potential mentors and/or high-profile influencers, and
- ✓ Reverse your limiting beliefs by turning your <u>past</u> into your **power**.

Filled with inspiring quotes and potentially life-changing exercises, *The Life You Want Workbook* is the ultimate resource for developing a bulletproof action plan and creating the life you ultimately want.

www.danmcdaniel.net/workbook

Extreme Honesty
Reflections of a Nineteen-Year-Old Philosopher

"It's one of the best books on success I have ever read."
—Alex Hamm, Founder, Attitudes 4 Innovation.com, The #1 Source for Mindset Design

"I found this book to be extraordinarily insightful."
—Mark Raciappa, CEO, ActionCOACH, The World's #1 Business Coaching Firm

THE BOOK THAT REVOLUTIONIZED THE SELF-PUBLISHING INDUSTRY

Honesty is the responsibility of making the best use of what you have—your mind, your talents, your abilities, and time—in order to lead a successful, fulfilling life of realized potential. An instant classic, *Extreme Honesty* takes the reader on a journey of self-discovery through revolutionary principles for overcoming fear, adversity, and conformity. Containing timeless aphorisms and the groundbreaking narrative, *The Allegory of Excellence*, this book shows you how gaining self-education, using the time value of wisdom, and thinking like a corporation can make you nonpareil—unrivaled and transcendent among your peers.

In this intellectual manifesto, the author shares the fundamentals that took him from a life of poverty to affluence, from obesity to fitness, from timid to courageous, from depression to fulfillment, and from mediocrity to achievement. Practiced consistently, the philosophy of extreme honesty will help you rapidly reach the top of your industry, achieve childhood dreams, and ultimately realize that the sky… is no longer the limit.

www.danmcdaniel.net/honesty

Bibliography

Chapter 1: Vision

"Criss Angel." *E! True Hollywood Story*. E! Entertainment Television. 24 June 2009. Television.

Nightingale, Earl. *The Strangest Secret*. Nightingale-Conant, 1956.

Tracy, Brian. "Secrets of Self-Made Millionaires." Better Life Media. 2004.

Vanzant, Iyanla. "What Saved Iyanla Vanzant's Life." *Super Soul Sunday*. Oprah Winfrey Network. 3 June 2012. Television.

Chapter 2: Purpose

"Comfort." *Oxford Pocket Dictionary of Current English*. Oxford University Press, 2015. Web.

"Conformity." *Oxford Pocket Dictionary of Current English*. Oxford University Press, 2015. Web.

Forleo, Marie. Interview by Soren Gordhamer. "Building a Business from the Inside Out: A Soulful Approach to Entrepreneurship." Wisdom 2.0, 2014. Web. 13 November 2014.

Frankl, Viktor. *Man's Search for Meaning*. Boston: Beacon Press, 2006.

McDaniel, Dan. *Extreme Honesty: Reflections of a Nineteen-Year-Old Philosopher*. 2013.

Minaj, Nicki. Interview by Dasha Ware. *MEE Magazine*. 2008. Web. 28 September 2008.

Bibliography

Minaj, Nicki. Interview by Ellen DeGeneres. *The Ellen DeGeneres Show*. 2011. Web. 10 January 2011.

Minaj, Nicki. Interview by Jabari. I Am Jabari. 2009. Web. 10 August 2009.

Minaj, Nicki. Interview by Ray Daniels. A-105 Radio. Web.

Nicki Minaj: My Time Now. MTV. 28 November 2010. Television.

Nightingale, Earl. *Lead the Field*. Nightingale-Conant, 1987.

Pink, Daniel. *Drive: The Surprising Truth About What Motivates Us*. New York: Riverhead Books, 2011.

Chapter 3: Relationships

"About EOFire." EOFire. <http://www.eofire.com/about/>.

"About Ryan Holiday." Ryan Holiday. <http://www.ryanholiday.net/about/>.

"Arnold's Blueprint." *30 for 30 Shorts*. ESPN Films. 26 September 2012. Television.

"Arnold Schwarzenegger." *Biography*. A&E Television Networks. 1997. Television.

"Arnold Schwarzenegger Biography." Arnold Schwarzenegger. <http://www.schwarzenegger.com/bio>.

"Billboard Biz: Current Boxscore." Billboard. 24 September 2013. <http://www.billboard.com/biz/current-boxscore>.

Britton, Felicity. *Nicki Minaj: Conquering Hip-Hop*. Minneapolis: Twenty-First Century Books, 2013.

Burns, Stephanie. "7 Reasons to Join a Mastermind Group." Forbes. 21 October 2013. <http://www.forbes.com/sites/chicceo/2013/10/21/7-reasons-to-join-a-mastermind-group/#71eea47817ab>.

Caetano, Sandy. "Trish Stratus: It's Stratus-fying Being on Top." *Top Choice Magazine*. 5 May 2011. <http://www.topchoicemagazine.com/articles/trish-stratus-its-status-fying-being-top>.

"Calculate Your Body Mass Index." National Heart, Lung, and Blood Institute. <http://www.nhlbi.nih.gov/health/educational/lose_wt/BMI/bmicalc.htm>.

Caramanica, Jon. "For Young Superstar Taylor Swift, Big Wins Mean Innocence Lost." *The New York Times* 2 February 2010. C5. <http://www.nytimes.com>.

Caulfield, Keith. "Official: Taylor Swift's '1989' Debuts with 1.287 Million Sold in First Week." Billboard. 4 November 2014. <http://www.billboard.com/articles/columns/chart-beat/6304536/official-taylor-swifts-1989-debuts-with-1287-million-sold-in>.

Bibliography

"EOFire's Income Reports." EOFire. <http://www.eofire.com/income/>.

"Ep 49: Tim Answers Your 10 Most Popular Questions." *The Tim Ferriss Show*. iTunes. 11 December 2014. Podcast.

"Eventual Millionaire Testimonial." Jaime Tardy. 12 September 2013.

Ferrazzi, Keith. *Never Eat Alone: And Other Secrets to Success, One Relationship at a Time*. New York: Crown Business, 2005.

Ferriss, Tim. Interview by Steve Harrison and Jack Canfield. "How to Write a Best-Selling Book." Tim Ferriss, 2012. Web. 11 September 2012.

"From Mentee to Millionaire - $2 Million Cash in Less Than 2 Years with My Client John Lee Dumas." *Eventual Millionaire*. iTunes. 2 February 2015. Podcast.

Greene, Robert, and 50 Cent. *The 50th Law*. New York: G-Unit Books, 2009.

Hill, Napoleon. *Think and Grow Rich*. Meriden: The Ralston Society, 1937.

Hoehn, Charlie. "12 Lessons Learned While Marketing 'The 4-Hour Body.'" Tim Ferriss: The 4-Hour Workweek. 10 March 2011. <http://www.fourhourworkweek.com/2011/03/10/12-lessons-learned-while-marketing-the-4-hour-body/>.

Hoehn, Charlie. "About Charlie." Charlie Hoehn. <http://www.charliehoehn.com/about/>.

Hoehn, Charlie. *Recession-Proof Graduate: How to Land the Job You Want by Doing Free Work*. Hoehn Zone Media, 2014.

Holiday, Ryan. Interview by Brian Rose. "Ryan Holiday - Trust Me, I'm Lying." London Real, 2014. Web. 8 June 2014.

Holiday, Ryan. Interview by Charlie Houpert. "Ryan Holiday on How to Get an Education." Kickass Academy, 2013. Web. 24 September 2013.

Holiday, Ryan. Interview by Maneesh Sethi. "Ryan Holiday and Guerilla Marketing." Hack the System with Maneesh Sethi, 2013. Web. 14 January 2013.

"Infographic." Eventual Millionaire. <http://www.eventualmillionaire.com/infographic/>.

"Jennifer Lopez Honored with 2,500th Star on the Hollywood Walk of Fame." Walk of Fame. 20 June 2013.

Krohn, Katherine E. *Oprah Winfrey: Global Media Leader*. Minneapolis: Twenty-First Century Books, 2009.

Lakhiani, Vishen. "7 Lessons from Building a $15-Million-Per-Year Lifestyle Business with No Loans, VCs, or Angel Money." Mindvalley Insights. 14 December 2012. <http://www.mindvalleyinsights.com/7-lessons-from-building-a-lifestyle-business/>.

Bibliography

Lakhiani, Vishen. Interview by Andrew Warner. "How Mindvalley Founder Built a $40M Company With Only $700." Mixergy, 2013. Web. 30 October 2013.

Leonard, Devin. "Taylor Swift *Is* the Music Industry." Bloomberg. 12 November 2014. <http://www.bloomberg.com/bw/articles/2014-11-12/taylor-swift-and-big-machine-are-the-music-industry>.

Lopez, Jennifer. Interview by Hoda Kotb. "Jennifer Lopez in a Candid and Revealing Look at the Most Defining Moments of Her Life." 92Y, 2014. Web. 12 November 2014.

"Mentor." *Merriam-Webster's Collegiate® Dictionary, Eleventh Edition*. Merriam-Webster, 2015. Web.

Milligan, Jonathan. "How to Launch a Successful Mastermind Group." Michael Hyatt. <http://www.michaelhyatt.com/launch-a-mastermind.html>.

Minaj, Nicki. Interview by Elliott Wilson. "CRWN with Elliott Wilson Ep. 15: Nicki Minaj." WatchLOUD, 2014. Web. 18 December 2014.

"Nicki Minaj Signs with Young Money/Universal." *XXL Magazine*. 31 August 2009. <http://www.xxlmag.com/xxl-magazine/2009/08/xxclusive-nicki-minaj-officially-signs-with-young-money/>.

"Ryan Holiday: 'The Obstacle is the Way.'" Talks at Google. 28 May 2014.

Savara, Sid. "How to Start and Run a Mastermind Group." Lifehack. <http://www.lifehack.org/articles/featured/how-to-start-and-run-a-mastermind-group.html>.

Schneider, Marc. "Taylor Swift Named Billboard Woman of the Year." Billboard. 11 October 2011. <http://www.billboard.com/articles/news/466285/taylor-swift-named-billboard-woman-of-the-year>.

Schwartzberg, Lauren. "Nicki Minaj's Former Manager Debra Antney Explains Why Nicki Is the Hardest Working Rapper Alive." Vice. 22 September 2014. <http://www.vice.com/read/nicki-minajs-former-manager-debra-antney-on-how-onika-tanya-maraj-became-the-best-rapper-alive-666>.

Schwarzenegger, Arnold. "Arnold's Perspectives." Arnold Schwarzenegger. 3 October 2001. <http://www.schwarzenegger.com>.

Schwarzenegger, Arnold. *Total Recall: My Unbelievably True Life Story*. New York: Fitness Publications, 2012.

Sokol, Jacob. "Sensophy Inner Circle." Sensophy. <http://www.sensophy.com/inner-circle/>.

Tardy, Jaime. *The Eventual Millionaire: How Anyone Can Be an Entrepreneur and Successfully Grow Their Startup*. Hoboken: John Wiley & Sons, 2014.

Bibliography

"Taylor Swift." *CNN Spotlight*. Cable News Network. 14 November 2014. Television.

"Taylor Swift." *E! Entertainment Special*. E! Entertainment Television. 1 December 2010. Television.

"Taylor Swift Named IFPI Global Recording Artist of 2014." IFPI. 23 February 2015. <http://www.ifpi.org/news/Taylor-Swift-named-IFPI-global-recording-artists-of-2014>.

"Taylor Swift Wins CMA Entertainer of the Year." Fox News. 11 November 2009. <http://www.foxnews.com/entertainment/2009/11/11/taylor-swift-wins-cma-entertainer-year/>.

"The Theory of Awesomeness." Awesomeness Fest. 13 August 2013.

Todd, Anne M. *Tyra Banks: Model and Talk Show Host*. New York: Infobase Publishing, 2009.

"Tyra Banks." *Biography*. A&E Television Networks. 2 February 2012. Television.

"Tyra Banks Biography." A&E Television Networks. <http://www.biography.com/people/tyra-banks-16242328>.

"Tyra Banks." *E! Entertainment Special*. E! Entertainment Television. 28 September 2011. Television.

"Zentrepreneur for Startups." Zentrepreneur. <http://www.zentrepreneur.com/for-startups>.

Chapter 4: Beliefs

Orman, Suze. Interview by Nancy Harrington. "Suze Orman Interview." The Archive of American Television, 2012. Web. 18 October 2012.

Orman, Suze. "Personal Finance with Suze Orman." AOL Build, 2015. Web. 12 March 2015.

"You Become What You Believe." Oprah's Lifeclass Webcast. 13 October 2011.

Chapter 5: Action

"Big Sean on How He Met Kanye West." Vlad TV. 3 May 2011.

"Colin Wright - Extreme Lifestyle Experiments." TEDx Talks. 17 February 2011.

"How I Got Signed." Endangered Creations. 15 December 2008.

Lacy, Eric. "Detroit rapper, Kanye West protégé Big Sean admits first album was a flop." MLive. 8 August 2012. <http://www.mlive.com/entertainment/detroit/index.ssf/2012/08/detroit_rapper_kanye_west_prot.html>.

Bibliography

Sean, Big. Interview by Nick Huff Barili and Mark Jenkins. "Big Sean talks Kanye West, Being Broke, and Freestyling with Pharrell." Hard Knock TV, 2011. Web. 11 January 2011.

Chapter 6: Habits

Guillebeau, Chris. "About The Art of Non-Conformity." Chris Guillebeau. <http://www.chrisguillebeau.com/about/>.

Guillebeau, Chris. "Books." Chris Guillebeau. <http://www.chrisguillebeau.com/books/>.

Guillebeau, Chris. "How to Write 300,000 Words in One Year." Chris Guillebeau. 26 September 2011. <http://www.chrisguillebeau.com/how-to-write-300000-words-in-1-year/>.

Guillebeau, Chris. *The $100 Startup: Reinvent the Way You Make a Living, Do What You Love, and Create a New Future*. New York: Crown Business, 2012.

Guillebeau, Chris. *The Art of Non-Conformity: Set Your Own Rules, Live the Life You Want, and Change the World*. New York: TarcherPerigee, 2010.

"Habit." *American Heritage® Dictionary of the English Language, Fifth Edition*. Houghton Mifflin Harcourt Publishing Company, 2011. Web.

Hardy, Darren. *The Compound Effect*. New York: Vanguard Press, 2010.

Tzu, Lao. Translation by Derek Lin. *Tao Te Ching: Annotated & Explained*. SkyLight Paths, 2006.

Chapter 7: Momentum

"Jennifer Lopez Biography." IMDb. <http://www.imdb.com/name/nm0000182/bio>.

"Jennifer Lopez (Ep. 215)." *Behind the Music*. VH1. 8 July 2010. Television.

"Jennifer Lopez: Her Life. Her Journey." NUVOtv. 18 July 2013. Television.

Chapter 8: Patience

"Dennis Swanson Named Executive Vice President, Chief Operating Officer of the Viacom Television Stations Group." PR Newswire. 15 July 2002. <http://www.prnewswire.com/news-releases/dennis-swanson-named-executive-vice-president-chief-operating-officer-of-the-viacom-television-stations-group-76192797.html>.

Gladwell, Malcolm. *Outliers: The Story of Success*. New York: Little, Brown, and Company, 2008.

Greene, Robert. *Mastery*. New York: Penguin Group, 2012.

"How Oprah Overcame Her 'Lonely' Childhood." *The Oprah Winfrey Show*. Oprah Winfrey Network. 15 July 2015. Web.

"Meet the Man Who Discovered Oprah." *The Oprah Winfrey Show*. Oprah Winfrey Network. 8 May 2015. Web.

"Oprah: 'My Broadcasting Career Started at the Church.'" *The Oprah Winfrey Show*. Oprah Winfrey Network. 5 August 2015. Web.

"Oprah's Original Audition Tape." *The Oprah Winfrey Show*. Oprah Winfrey Network. 5 May 2014. Web.

"Oprah Wasn't Voted Most Likely to Succeed in High School." *The Oprah Winfrey Show*. Oprah Winfrey Network. 21 July 2015. Web.

Swanson, Dennis. Interview by Dean Ken Freeman. "Discovering Oprah: Chicago's WLS-TV Morning Talk Show." Boston University School of Management, 2012. Web. 3 October 2012.

The Oprah Winfrey Show: 20th Anniversary Collection. Paramount, 2005. DVD.

Winfrey, Oprah. Interview by Amanda Facelle. "Oprah Winfrey on Career, Life, and Leadership." Stanford Graduate School of Business, 2014. Web. 28 April 2014.

Chapter 9: Failure

Andriani, Lynn. "The Dollars and Sense of Suze Orman." *Publishers Weekly*. 24 February 2003. <http://www.publishersweekly.com/pw/print/20030224/28423-the-dollars-and-sense-of-suze-orman.html>.

Bernstein, Jacob. "Suze Orman's Finest Hour." Upstart Business Journal. 30 March 2009. <http://www.upstart.bizjournals.com/executives/2009/03/30/Suze-Orman-Profile.html?page=all>.

"Bestselling Books of the Year, 1996-2007." Publishers Weekly. 24 March 2008. <http://www.publishersweekly.com/pw/by-topic/industry-news/publishing-and-marketing/article/2110-bestselling-books-of-the-year-1996-2007.html>.

"Books and Tapes." Suze Orman Media. <http://www.suzeorman.com/about-suze/books-and-tapes/>.

Carvajal, Doreen. "The Little Bookshop in Your Living Room; Publishers Find New Market Through Television Shopping Network." *The New York Times*. 14 February 1998. <http://www.nytimes.com/1998/02/14/business/little-bookshop-your-living-room-publishers-find-new-market-through-television.html?pagewanted=all>.

Bibliography

Downey, Kevin. "Suze Orman is Going from Saturday's CNBC Finale to Daytime TV's Money Wars." TV First Look. 27 March 2015. <http://www.tvfirstlook.com/2015/03/qa-5qs-on-friday-cnbc-suze-orman-show-suze-ormans-money-wars/>.

"Failure." *Merriam-Webster*. 2015. Web.

Frick, Robert. "If You Knew Suze…" *Kiplinger's Personal Finance* (November 1998): 96-102.

Orman, Suze. Interview by Ernie Manouse. "Suze Orman on InnerVIEWS with Ernie Manouse." Houston PBS, 2011. Web. 28 February 2011.

Orman, Suze. Interview by Korina Sanchez. "ANC Up Close and Personal with Suze Orman: A Korina Sanchez Interview." ANC, 2012. Web. 9 March 2012.

Chapter 10: Persistence

"About Tyler Perry." Tyler Perry Studios. <http://www.tylerperry.com/biography/>.

"And the Grammy Went to… Kanye West." The Recording Academy. 09 March 2012. <http://www.grammy.com/news/and-the-grammy-went-to-kanye-west>.

Casey, Nora. "Tyler Perry Biography." Encyclopedia Britannica. <http://www.britannica.com/biography/Tyler-Perry>.

"Gold & Platinum: Searchable Database." The Recording Industry Association of America. <http://www.riaa.com/gold-platinum/>.

Horowitz, Steven. "Notorious B.I.G. Autopsy Report Released." HipHopDX. 7 December 2012. <http://www.hiphopdx.com/news/id.22133/title.notorious-big-autopsy-report-relesaed>.

Hughes, Zondra. "How Tyler Perry Rose from Homelessness to a $5 Million Mansion." *Ebony* (January 2004): 86-92.

"Interview with Tyler Perry; Dolly Parton Speaks Out." *Larry King Live*. Cable News Network. 20 February 2009. Television.

"Jay-Z – The Blueprint." Discogs. <http://www.discogs.com/Jay-Z-The-Blueprint/release/251894>.

"Kanye West." *Driven*. VH1. 24 September 2005. Television.

"Kim Kardashian, Kanye West Welcome Baby Daughter." The Hollywood Reporter. 15 June 2013. <http://www.hollywoodreporter.com/news/kim-kardashian-kanye-west-welcome-569441>.

Bibliography

Montgomery, James. "Kanye Scores 10 Grammy Nominations; Usher and Alicia Keys Land Eight." Viacom International. 7 December 2004. <http://www.mtv.com/news/1494569/kanye-scores-10-grammy-nominations-usher-and-alicia-keys-land-eight/>.

Newman, Jason. "Kanye West Co-Writer Says New Album is 'Like a Pair of Timberlands.'" Rolling Stone. 6 October 2014. <http://www.rollingstone.com/music/news/kanye-west-co-writer-says-new-album-is-like-a-pair-of-timberlands-20141006>.

Pareles, Jon. "Eazy-E, 31, Performer Who Put Gangster Rap on the Charts." *The New York Times*. 28 March 1995. <http://www.nytimes.com/1995/03/28/obituaries/eazy-e-31-performer-who-put-gangster-rap-on-the-charts.html>.

"Persistence." *Oxford American College Dictionary*. Oxford University Press, 2015. Web.

Pullery, Brett. "A Showbiz Whiz." Forbes. 15 September 2005. <http://www.forbes.com/forbes/2005/1003/075.html>.

Reid, Shaheem. "Kanye West Injured in L.A. Accident." Viacom International. 23 October 2002. <http://www.mtv.com/news/1458308/kanye-west-injured-in-la-accident/>.

"Tyler Perry Biography." A&E Television Networks. <http://www.biography.com/people/tyler-perry-361274#related-video-gallery>.

Winfrey, Oprah. "Oprah Interviews Tyler Perry." *O, The Oprah Winfrey Magazine*. December 2010. <http://www.oprah.com/entertainment/Oprah-Interviews-Tyler-Perry_1>.

About the Author

DAN MCDANIEL is a Microsoft® Certified Professional, 4-time Business Achievement Award recipient, Horatio Alger Association of Distinguished Americans scholar, former chapter president and national delegate of Future Business Leaders of America, and former spokesperson for the Environmental Protection Agency's "It's My Environment" Earth Day initiative. He has been featured in several magazines, including *Tomorrow's Business Leader* and the *Louisiana Leader*. An emerging television personality, he has appeared on CNBC's *The Suze Orman Show* and starred in MTV's Emmy Award-winning documentary series *True Life*.

At age 19, Dan McDaniel walked away from over $100,000 in scholarships and grants from Louisiana State University's E.J. Ourso College of Business to become a professional writer. He has used the principles in this book to lose 90 pounds, meet Oprah Winfrey, and fulfill his lifelong dream of becoming a bestselling author. His major definite purpose is to help you achieve your goals and create the life you truly want.

You can learn more about him (and discover how he can help *you*) by visiting **www.danmcdaniel.net**.

37110241R00076

Made in the USA
San Bernardino, CA
10 August 2016